RETURNING
Duski's Story

by Susan White-Bowden

GATEWAY PRESS, INC.
Baltimore, MD   2004

Copyright © 2004 by
Susan White-Bowden
All rights reserved.

Permission to reproduce in any form
must be secured from the author.

Please direct all correspondence and book orders to:
Susan White-Bowden
2863 Benson Rd.
Finksburg, MD 21048

Library of Congress Control Number 2004103324
ISBN 0-9633762-5-X

Published for the author by
Gateway Press, Inc.
1001 N. Calvert Street
Baltimore, MD 21202-3897

www.Gatewaypress.com

Printed in the United States of America

FOR JODY

WITH THANKS:

To The Laverys: Judi, Phil, Erin, Christy, Isabelle and Jack. For sharing their wonderful beach house with us. I know in my heart that there is no place else on this earth where I could have written this book.

And to my husband, Jack, for being there with me and for me and once again being my colleague in the, sometimes painful, always invasive process of writing about our personal lives.

Other books by Susan White-Bowden

Everything to Live For

From A Healing Heart

Moonbeams Come At Dark Times

The Barn Cat, Sassy and A Guardian Angel: Heroic Animal Tales

Off-Season: Living the Retirement Dream
By Susan White-Bowden & Jack Bowden

TABLE OF CONTENTS

PROLOGUE viii
CHAPTER ONE 1
    Summer 1977
CHAPTER TWO 13
    Dewey Beach, Delaware
    Fall 2001 – The Present
CHAPTER THREE 19
    The Beach
    2001 – The Present
CHAPTER FOUR 23
CHAPTER FIVE 29
    California
    Summer 1978
CHAPTER SIX 37
    The Farm
    2001
CHAPTER SEVEN 45
    The Farm
    August 1979
CHAPTER EIGHT 51
    The Apartment
    1980
CHAPTER NINE 61
    The Farm
    November 2001 – The Present

CHAPTER TEN 67
　　The Beach
　　November 30, 2001
CHAPTER ELEVEN 77
　　Ocean City, Maryland
　　1984
CHAPTER TWELVE 83
　　The Beach
　　2001 – The Present
CHAPTER THIRTEEN 95
　　The Farm
　　Summer 1990
CHAPTER FOURTEEN 99
　　The Farm
　　2001
CHAPTER FIFTEEN 105
　　September 2002
CHAPTER SIXTEEN 113
　　The Beach
　　October 2002
AFTERWORD 123
　　About Beliefs
FINAL WORD 129
　　The Farm
　　Winter 2004
Author Recommended Books 131
Picture Information & Identification 133

PROLOGUE

It has been almost a decade since I first began exploring what many others accept on faith, but about which I had serious doubts. Today, my heart has come to believe what my mind still questions. After you hear my story perhaps you'll understand.

I've always believed that we are born with the free will to use our God-given abilities to shape our destiny, through determination and commitment. However, many believe that our lives, even our deaths, are largely, although not completely, predetermined. And that if we don't accomplish what we are suppose to, in this life, then we must try again in another.

It is because of my son that I became interested in this philosophy, and the question that still haunts me: Why hadn't I been able to keep him alive?

Surviving his death took a great deal of help from the people around me, and all the courage and strength I could muster. One source of comfort was this spiritual belief that I came to embrace at that time. It was a quiet comfort that didn't need explanation, or acknowledgment and approval from others, to ease my pain.

But with the passage of time, almost twenty years after I buried my son, I found myself wanting to have reason attached to my beliefs and felt compelled to give in to my spiritual curiosity, challenge my fears, and seek a better understanding of both life and death. And so, in 1994 I had my astrology chart done by karmic astrologer Linda Brady, who is internationally recognized in this field. She is also a holistic teacher who, along with her husband Michael Brady, founded Creative Choices, a holistic educational center based in Baltimore. Linda was recommended to me by a Baltimore publishing executive.

Linda Brady's background impressed and intrigued me. She has a bachelor's degree in psychology, and a masters in educational administration. Her religious education took place in the Episcopal Church and at a Catholic College, and although she believed in God and the teachings of Christ, and still does, she says, "I wanted to know why things happened, the purpose of things. I never got the answers I was seeking. I wanted to know about the inequities of life; why some people were gifted and others were not; why some people had IQs of 10 and others 140? Why does this happen? A priest would say, 'You have to have faith, my child, in God's plan.' That just wasn't good enough for me."

Linda began to study astrology, and it was in that quest that she not only found the answers she'd been seeking, but astrology opened the doors to many more questions, about life and purpose and reason, that she felt she needed to have answered in order to be satisfied spiritually as well as intellectually.

"You find the right questions,' Linda explains, "and the answers, revealing truth, will come. Socrates said that, that's how he taught.

"Astrology gave me a language to visualize and bring concept to life's experiences. Eventually it led me to a belief in reincarnation, and an understanding of my soul. Not all astrologers believe in reincarnation—I didn't at first. The whole idea of soul creation came later. Soul personality integration is a function of years of doing this work—and the soul is a real energy, not just a theoretical thing—a real tangible part of my life—and astrology started me on the path to that. There is nothing now that I can't find meaning in."

Over the years she not only became a devout believer in karmic astrology but a counselor and teacher as well. In the book that she co-authored with writer Evan St. Lifer, *Discovering Your Soul Mission*, she describes the difference between traditional astrology and karmic astrology. "While traditional astrology implies that we abdicate responsibility for what befalls us to the cosmos, karmic astrology equips us with the understanding to shape our life the way we want it to be."

I liked that difference; it eased many of my doubts.

I had a private session with Linda in the softly lit counseling room of her home. There was a large comfortable sofa, two chairs, a fireplace, and interesting paintings, surely symbolic of astrology, hanging on the walls. But I was drawn to the lion statues on the mantle and a nearby table because I already knew I was born under the sun sign of Leo. Linda told me that, although she was born under the sun sign of Sagittarius, her north node, or soul potential, is in Leo, which she explained, pertains to her soul mission in this lifetime. I felt confused and knew it would take some study to understand any of it.

"Tell me something about yourself," she began, "tell me why you are here?"

"Why don't you tell me about me," I said with a smile, but there was an edge to my voice similar to the one I might use as a skeptical reporter. She knew that I was questioning her ability to read my life from the chart she had in front of her. It had been prepared from the information concerning the date, time and place of my birth that I'd given her when I made the appointment.

I was sure she had seen doubtful clients many times before; people suspecting that this was some kind of parlor game or trick used to tell me things only I could know. But since my husband, Jack Bowden, and I had been on Baltimore television for twenty-some years, and I had written three non-fiction books about my life and family relationships, including the suicides of both my son Jody White, in

1977, and his father two years earlier, there wasn't much she, or anyone else, couldn't know.

Linda readily acknowledged that she knew about my life from my career, she called herself "a fan." But she said she had not had a chance to read any of my books. I suspended my mistrust and suspicion and willed myself to be more receptive. Otherwise, I figured, I was wasting her time and my money.

A candle on the coffee table threw flickering shadows across her pleasantly pretty, almost cameo-like face. Her blonde hair lay smoothly at the sides of her head, curving in a blunt cut under her chin. Her soft accepting, non-critical eyes drew me in.

She read from the astrological chart as if it were a map of my present life and what she said were my past lives. (I hadn't written a book about that.) And she said it showed where my life was headed—my north node.

"Your north node is in the sign of Scorpio and you come from Taurus. Scorpio is the energy of life and death, re-transformation—it is that intense—it's that passionate—it's that powerful. It's always dealing with regeneration; it's always dealing with transformation. It looks like sometimes it's dealing in chaos. What it's doing is creating order from chaos. It has this really strong bias toward understanding death—the mystery of death and what happens after death. It is the energy of the mystic in the most powerful intense ways. It causes and creates tragedy because it needs to—that's how it learns. It primarily learns from death experiences because it understands that life is a question of living and dying and being re-born—EVERY DAY—every-single-day."

Linda became more animated as she spoke with increasing certainty.

"It would be the process of your life, and in doing that you would prepare yourself to become *exactly what you are*, which is a leader in transformational experience. When you had a tragedy, you took it to the world, and in taking it to the world you became a teacher to the world, and in doing it out of pain, out of emotional pain, it allowed other people to connect with that emotional pain. You didn't hide it—you didn't step away from it—you were a presence. Scorpio will do that—Scorpio at its best is the sign of the spiritual counselor—the energy of a person who can touch someone else's soul.

"Now, you don't come from that. You come from lifetimes where things were pretty secure. You didn't like change and would do anything to avoid it. In this life you need to learn to accept change, no matter what the consequences."

I thought about my first marriage and how I stayed in it for twenty years even though I was very unhappy for most of those years. Finally I had established myself in a career and felt strong enough to get a divorce. Later when I refused a reconciliation, my ex-husband killed himself and I felt guilty and responsible for his death.

Although enthralled by hearing reason and purpose being attached to my life, and my losses, I was anxious to hear what Linda could tell me about my son and my second husband, Jack. I had also given her birth information for them and she had prepared their charts as well. Knowing that I only had an hour for this session I urged her on.

"Tell me about Jody's chart."

"Jody was—is—a very strong Piscean personality. Not only did he have two planets in Pisces he also had a 12th house in Pisces and," her voice rose with surprise and revelation, "he had a south node in Pisces. He was loaded with Pisces. What that means is that Jody—without trying to sound tacky— almost had an angelic process going. He was almost not the kind of person or the kind of personality that you would expect to come to this plane. People like Jody never quite fit in. They are never quite comfortable here. They come here for someone else—to come and create a connection. They come as gifts. But I think on some deep, deep level that are not meant to stay.

"It's almost as if the timing was wrong," then her voice rising again, "or very right. Jody was like an incarnated angel saying, 'I'll be here for X amount of time and then I'll go home.' She paused, gazing at me, 'And then I'll come back. But if I come back it will be for you Mom, or you or you.'

"Piscean people are creative, artistic. They're gentle, sensitive—too sensitive. Pisceans are the mystics of the universe. Do you think you had known Jody in another lifetime?"

I was choked with emotion and could barely answer. "I don't know, we were very, very close from the day he was born. We seemed to have a special connection right from the start."

Linda nodded, "He was your soul mate. You had known each other in many lifetimes. Jody had two soul missions for his short life. He needed to understand mother, and that kind of love, and he needed to awaken you to the powerful emotions of your soul mission, revealed in your north node of Scorpio—investigating the depths of your emotions and how to use them for self-healing and for helping others—transforming darkness into light."

Seeing that I was overcome with emotion, and being pulled toward deep introspection, Linda moved to the next chart without prompting.

"Jack! — shall I continue?"

I smiled, "Yes, Jack. He's hopeless—at least spiritually."

"Ah-h-h-," she responded, with the strength of deep personal understanding, "Jack is an Aquarian. I come from Aquarius, my south node is in Aquarius. I have lots of Aquarian energy. You see Aquarians have this thing —Aquarians are really rational and logical—da-da-da. We think we're so cool, because we don't believe in spiritual things. But the real thing Aquarians are doing... we're setting up that logical cool front because we're so scared. Inside we're going 'Oh God, oh God, oh God,' but we do the cool exterior so well nobody ever gets our game. Aquarians are very, very bright. He comes from Virgo which is another rational, analytical energy, so he's got a lot of it. He's a very bright man, rational, intellectual, he's quite cognizant. It's also a safe place for him to be."

As Linda spoke her eyes moved around the chart. Surprise, tempered with humor, and a note of regret came into her voice. "Oh my, Jack's north node, which reflects his soul mission or soul potential for this life is in Pisces. Jack's north node is where your son's south node was. Jody and Jack." She paused, continuing almost with sadness. "If Jody had stayed around longer he might have turned Jack around. Because Jack's soul mission in this life is to learn how to be more spiritual; to learn how to be emotional and sensitive and be comfortable with it—and to have faith. For Jack to do his north node he's going to have to let go of some of his cognition—that's what he's afraid of. He doesn't get that you can be intellectual, rational, cognizant and spiritual. He thinks you've got to go one way or the other—either/or—all or nothing."

Linda looked back at Jody's chart. "Jody definitely could have changed that way of thinking in Jack."

Linda paused, "Did Jody give you any warning?" I nodded my head. "What did he say?"

"He didn't say anything specifically. There were signs that he was giving up. My relationship with Jack was becoming more serious—we weren't married then, and Jody had become deeply involved with a girl—his first love. When she broke up with him—that was it. And, of course, there was the example his father had set. I guess thinking he'd lost everything— everyone—he killed himself."

Looking back at his chart, Linda explained that marriage and a family of his own were not what Jody had come here for. "He got what he came for," Linda said. "You gave him a good idea of what love is; in his next life he'll remember that. Does that make you feel better or worse?"

I shook my head, "I don't know," I didn't know. I felt that perhaps she had said that to make me feel better, to absolve me of any lingering feelings of guilt, of wishing that I had been able to keep him alive.

It was as if Linda were reading my mind. "If Jody had understood his soul potential in Virgo—at an early age, I mean by 10, or 11—and had understood that he didn't need to listen to his father about controlling emotions—and that he didn't need to follow him—maybe…"

She looked up from the chart and spoke with a sad softness not meant to accuse, "You know, Jody's north node or soul potential in Virgo is Jack's south node—Jack came from where Jody needed to go. Their soul patterns and missions are reversed. If they had really connected they could have definitely helped one another get to where each was intended to be in this life."

Linda saw the regret in my face, a regret that both Jack and I have felt about his lack of connection with Jody.

"But I don't know, Susan, I think Jody just needed to go home."

Linda paused again. The silence hung between us connecting our thoughts.

"Do you think you'll see Jody again?"

"Spiritually? I hope so, when I die."

"No, I mean here on earth? Do you think he'll incarnate during your lifetime?"

I smiled through my tears, "I think he already has."

> "Wherever we go, wherever we remain, the results of our actions follow us."
>
> The Buddha

CHAPTER ONE
Summer 1977

The car radio is playing that song again. The one that makes me think of Jody and cry. Not that I need a certain song, or a certain time of day, or the sound of a motorcycle, or seeing a teenage boy with his hair too long, to think of my son and how much I miss him.

It has been three months since his suicide. Three long months of endless sadness and tormented thoughts about the reasons. The break-up with his girl friend, the example of his father's suicide two-and-a-half years ago; my TV career—"Why hadn't I been home to save him? Why hadn't I known this was coming?"

"I think I'm going to love you for a long, long time," the words play out with the familiar melody. The tears turn to sobs.

At home my daughters are waiting for me; O'Donnell, 19, about to return to college, and Marjorie, 21, who will soon leave for California with her boyfriend. Shortly after the death of her father, Marjorie and a girl friend, who had just graduated from high school with her, had taken a backpacking trip in Europe and Africa. She needed to get away, a different environment—a change—time to reflect, I understood. I also understand the need now for her to go to California—for distance.

Jack's son Christopher, 7, is also there. It's summer, and there's no school, so he likes to stay with Marjorie and O'Donnell when he can. Jack will be there soon, for dinner. This time of grief has been so hard on him. He feels he failed my son; didn't work hard enough to get close; didn't try to be more like a father, fearing Jody would resent him, would think Jack was trying to take the place of his real dad, with whom he had been close.

And with me, he feels inadequate because he can't take this pain away. But what could he do? What could anybody do? All I want is my son back and nobody can give me that.

I'm also struggling with our relationship and he knows it. He knows I feel guilty; knows it's now hard for me to allow myself to love him. It seems so wrong. Every time I start to feel a little happy about something, a moment of pleasure, I stop myself—I don't deserve it; don't deserve any happiness. How dare I feel happy—how dare he feel happy—how can anyone feel happy? My son is dead.

Working together, as television reporters at the same TV station, has helped. It gives us daily contact, a chance, as colleagues, to share a common interest covering the news. And the fact that we have been friends for such a long time—long before we fell in love—has helped. Jack is my best friend, but even that doesn't seem right now; nothing does. I must try harder. I will tonight.

The sun is setting, and the stillness between daylight and darkness shrouds the old farm house. I sense without reason, something different about my homecoming this night. Anticipation replaces the dread of the past months. I walk quickly to the front door.

"Mom," shouts Marjorie with excitement, as I enter, "have we got a surprise for you!"

There it is on the sofa between Marjorie and Christopher. The boy has a big smile on his face. He is gently stroking and massaging a little dog; both hands buried in the thick, black wiry hair that covers her body. She seems delighted with the attention and the boy. Her adorable face, with its boxy nose, wild eyebrows over light brown eyes, is gazing up at me with expectation. She's young, but not a puppy; perhaps two or three months. The little dog jumps off the sofa, runs across the room, leaps into my arms, and frantically begins licking my face. I'm laughing so hard I'm crying. Everybody's laughing and talking at the same time.

"I looked outside and there she was," Marjorie stumbles over her words she's laughing so hard and is so excited.

"She was just sitting on the back steps. When I opened the door she just raced through the house—through the kitchen and dining room—through the living room and up

Returning

the stairs. She jumped on my bed and then went into O'Donnell's room and jumped on her bed with her."

O'Donnell is smiling and nodding her head. Marjorie rushes on, "She even ran up to the third floor, to Jody's room. It's like she's been here before—she knows where everything is and who we are."

"We can keep her, can't we?" Christopher says anxiously.

I look down at the little dog in my arms, into eyes that seem transparent enough to offer a path into her soul, yet piercing enough to see into mine.

"We'll have to check around and see if she belongs to anyone," I say, aware that I'm dreading that possibility. "Someone would be very sad to lose a dog like this."

Jack arrives and is delighted by the dog and the excitement she has engendered in all of us. After dinner he and Christopher leave, with more than the usual reluctance; the boy already feels attached to the dog and has to be pulled away with reassurances that he is certain to see it again. Jack shares custody of Christopher with his former wife, also named Susan, and this is one of her nights with their son. Susan and I have become friends, and I am grateful that she enthusiastically approves of my relationship with Jack and her son.

That night, climbing the stairs to go to bed, the little dog follows me. In the second floor hallway I pause, turn on the light switch to the third floor, and go up to Jody's room. It's become almost routine to do so; to see the room, his things—as if I'll finally wake up from this horrible nightmare and he'll be there. The little dog is at my heels.

I've kept the room as it was, the way Jody kept it; neat and orderly. His clothes are folded carefully in the built-in chest-of-drawers under the eaves. His tee-shirts, underwear and socks; his favorite sweater, shorts and pajamas; his torn jeans and old sweat pants that I was going to replace and throw away, until he died. And there is the wooden box under his bed. I pull it out, open it and look, almost every day, at the treasures he thought to save. The collection is diverse, but seems singular in revealing the boy who was my son. Organized precisely, in each of the eleven compartments, are such things as a perfectly coiled spool of yellow nylon cord; pad locks; old keys, to some other locks, hanging on a rawhide string. "What secrets could they unlock?" There is a neatly stacked deck of cards, and a metal mind teaser puzzle that no one else in the family could separate, but that Jody could undo very quickly with a couple rapid twists of his hands. Three colored light bulbs, red, blue and green, are grouped together in one corner of the box. He'd change the atmosphere in his room by using these color lights. It had seemed to me that the dimness they created darkened Jody's moods as well. Or was it something else that had altered his behavior. The drugs that I wanted to deny had become part of his life.

One section of the box contains music tapes, electrical plugs, assorted bolts and screws, and gizmos, from what I don't know. But Jody did. They must have been important to him and so they are now important to me. On top of that grouping, a tube of "Clearasil," for his teenage acne, which was very mild. In the back of the box, lying on its side is an unopened bottle of exotic beer. "Where had he gotten it? What was he saving it for?"

There is also his last report card, as a Junior at Baltimore Polytechnic Institute. He was in the accelerated math program there known as the A-Course. All of his math grades on that report card are in the 90s. Jody had gotten a 100 on the exam for Advanced Algebra that last term. All his conduct and effort marks are excellent. That report card had given me false hopes that the problems in Jody's life were normal adolescent troubles that he'd get through. After all, if he was doing that well in school how serious could the other things be?

Next to the report card is the scheduled assignment slip to take his SATs. He never took those tests. The date on the form is for a week after he died. And there is his wallet, with his driver's license, classified for both car and motorcycle.

The walls of his room also reflect the boy, each poster and picture he taped up himself. No one else would have been so exact. Many of the photographs are mine; taken of him with his friends, his father; racing his motorcycle. They are pictures of ordinary life, now visible reminders of how extraordinarily important that life was to me.

Most of the pictures are candid shots because when I asked Jody to pose for pictures, as a teenager, he would hide behind his friends, duck just as the shutter clicked, or hold his hand over his face. Mostly it was done to tease me, rather than not wanting his picture taken or being ashamed of how he looked. When I did get a good shot, in spite of his antics or because he didn't know I was taking it, he'd often ask for a copy and put it on the wall of his room. I'd be pleased, and he'd be pleased at pleasing me. But he didn't want to show it. However, sometimes he couldn't stop himself. The impish behavior of childhood would well up in him. The full-lipped bow of his mouth would stretch into a lopsided grin, exposing his not quite straight teeth.

As a much smaller boy, both front teeth had been knocked out when he fell face down while ice skating. We found the teeth on the ice, and my father, a dentist, put them back in. The teeth reattached but weren't exactly straight. However, we all agreed, especially Jody, that they were straight enough. The idea of wearing braces didn't appeal to him at all.

He had been so brave that day, with a face full of blood. I thought about it whenever he smiled, even when he was trying not to laugh, perhaps especially then. He'd clench those teeth tightly together to hold back the boyish giggle that was rarely allowed to escape in adolescence. But it was there, in the back of his throat, wanting, even trying, to come out. His eyes would water with the laughter he was trying so hard to hold back, and if he wasn't careful he'd get so tickled he'd choke and the silliness would spill out.

Those were the happy times, so painful now in the recalling, because they are gone. But I go to his room to be with him; whatever mood or emotion or part of him I can find. At least there are his things, just where he left them.

But, tonight is different. I'm startled to see Jody's white cotton cap, with the Bell Helmet insignia on it, in the middle of the floor.

He always wore this hat at motorcycle races, when he removed his helmet between races. In fact he had started wearing it all the time around the house and the farm; everywhere except to school.

Jody was wearing it in the last picture ever taken of him. The film was still in the camera at the time of his death. The photo had been taken by his sister, O'Donnell, home from college, who had captured Jody and his girlfriend sitting out in the sun on the lawn in back of our house.

It had been a summer-like day in late April. They had skipped school, apparently with a severe case of spring fever and young love. I was at work and as is often the case in such events, I, the parent, knew nothing of this illegal day off. When the film was developed and I saw the expression on Jody's face, my heart, already so badly broken by his death, crumbled even more because of the pain Jody must have been feeling before he killed himself; pain born from a first love lost. In the picture his eyes are locked on the face of the girl beside him. In his eyes is devotion, worship, perhaps complete surrender. Two weeks later she had broken up with him, for what she said was the final time. The suicide note he left said, "I loved her too much."

In keeping Jody's room as he left it, the cap had been on the table next to his bed. And now it's on the floor. I bend down, pick it up and put if back in place.

The little dog jumps on the bed, looks me in the eye and wags her tail.

"You," I say with surprise, you moved that hat didn't you?"

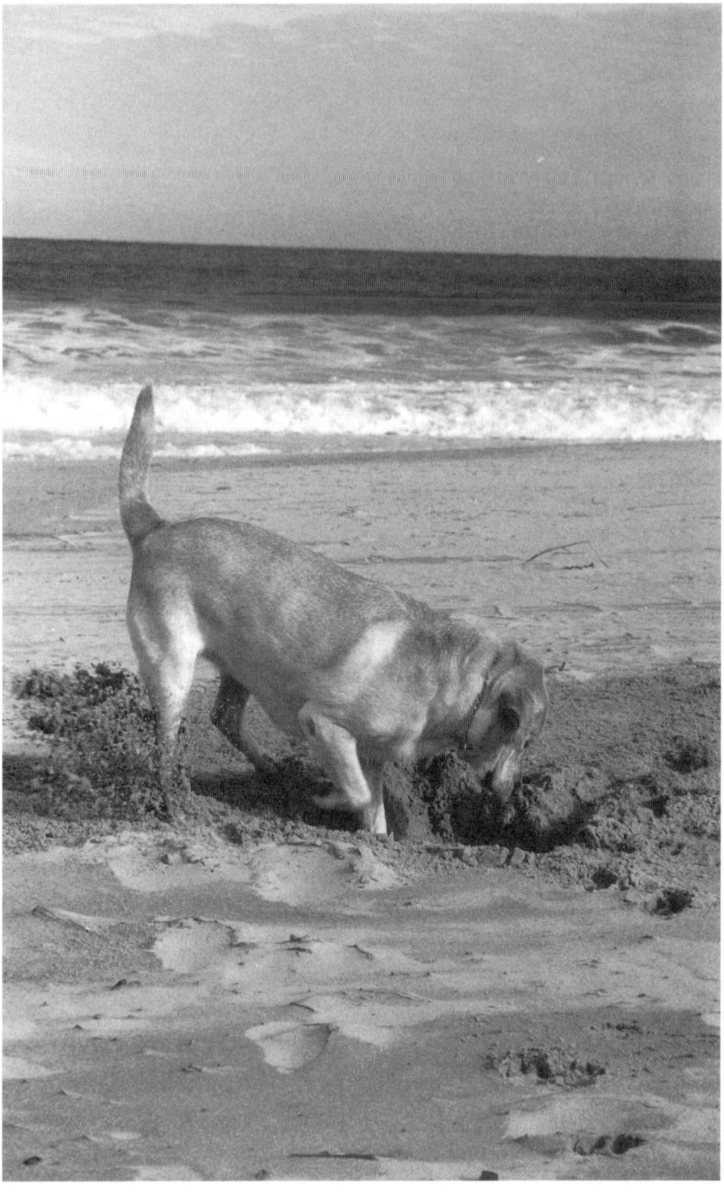

CHAPTER TWO
Dewey Beach, Delaware
Fall 2001 – Present Time

I've pulled my beach chair down close to the water. The waves are gentle and so is the breeze. It's a summer-like October day. The sun is warm but without the searing strength of August. Jack and I are back at our rented beach house for another glorious off-season stay. Our yellow lab, "Angel" digs in the sand nearby.

There's a little black terrier running down the beach by the water's edge, easily staying with the jogger by its side. The dog's short little legs, almost a blur, propel the little body at amazing speed. I'm wondering if our lab could move as fast. The little dog's floppy ears, that hang below the elongated head, beat out the rhythm of the gait. "So like our Duski Dog," I think with a smile. We have friends who called Duski the Dr. Seuss dog, because of her boxy head that seemed too big and legs that seemed too short. I wave to the dog's owner as they run by, recalling all those summers in Ocean City with Duski, running the beach with Jack.

Returning

Sharing the beach with little Duski Dog had meant so much to me. In the summer of 1980, the year after Jack and I were married, we rented an apartment in Ocean City that didn't allow pets, and we went on vacation without her. I was miserable. So sad was I that one morning, very early, Jack slipped out of bed, and without telling me where he was going he drove the three hours back to Baltimore, got Duski, then drove three more hours back to the beach with our little dog. When the owners of the apartment found out that we had a dog staying there we had to pay to have the place fumigated—but it was worth it. I've never loved Jack more, and I've never had a better vacation. It was during that vacation that we decided to buy a condo so we could take Duski, and her daughter Blaze, whenever we went to the beach—and for eight years we all enjoyed our "Oceanside Dog House."

Duski was an amazing dog. When did I suspect she was such a special being? Right away, I think, when I got home that day in the summer of 1977, and she was waiting with our children.

No one claimed her; no one had ever seen her before, and so Duski became part of our family; as easily as if she always had been.

It's hard now to remember exactly how we named her; she was black and she'd arrived about dusk, so Duski (with an i instead of a y) seemed to suit.

But it's impossible to find a word to describe what she did for me during that period in my life. I embraced her companionship without reserve. I've had many wonderful animal companions during my lifetime, as a child and as an adult—dogs, cats, ponies and horses—but the relationship with Duski was unlike any of the others.

I took her *everywhere*. At Channel 2 she spent hours by my desk as I typed and edited my stories and, except during the heat of summer, she usually went with me in the car. I'd park in the shade, leave the windows partially open, and walk her frequently. In the station parking lot my car provided Duski with a dog's-eye view of the world of TV and the characters it attracts. She'd sit for hours on the ledge at the back window and watch the people come and go; those who worked at the station and those who came to be on television, from local politicians to movie stars.

Duski became identified with me. If I took my car out to cover a story, often needing to meet a news cameraman coming from another assignment, my dog went with me. Notes to her and sometimes to me—mostly her—started appearing, tucked under the wiper blades on the car's windshield. I'd find them in the theater district, the state capital, in Baltimore's newly renovated Inner Harbor; the locations grew as Duski's notoriety did. "Hi Susan's dog, I wish I got to travel as much as you do." or "How come we never see you on TV?"

Duski seemed to enjoy being part of my professional life. It was when I left her home that she got upset and would throw a fit, usually emptying trash cans and spreading trash on the kitchen or bathroom floors. She never did that any other time. It was as if she were punishing me for not taking her with me. And although I never spoke of it with anyone, I worried that if I didn't keep Duski with me she might suddenly disappear from my life, the same way...

Somehow, Duski seemed connected with Jody, and my daughter's comment stayed in my mind. "It's like she's been here before; she knows where everything is and who we are."

One day late in the fall, a few weeks after her arrival, Duski and I set out for a walk in the woods around the farm property that borders the Liberty Reservoir. I hadn't been out there since Jody's death. I hadn't had the energy or the desire.

Marjorie, her boyfriend, and their dog Jackson, a Doberman, had left for California. O'Donnell was back at college. I was missing them and I think Duski was too. She and Jackson had been pals from the first day she arrived. Jack and Christopher came out many week-ends, but for the most part it was now just the two of us. My mood was low, melancholy. I was close to tears.

Leaves covered the forest floor, the ferns had turned brown. Patches of grey sky and dark water flashed beyond the bare trees.

Duski, who had been walking quietly beside me, stopped. Staring into the woods, her body began to quiver and then with a sudden start she leaped forward, scattering leaves beneath her paws as she was set into motion, running as fast as she could. She turned sharply through a clump of trees and twisted with a jump in the other direction. "She must have gotten the scent of a rabbit," I thought. "She must have some hunting dog blood in her background."

The chase was on. Through a bramble of bushes that had grown over the trail that summer, then down over the hill she went, around a turn and up a steep embankment.

She jumped into the air, as if launched, landing on a berm several feet away.

"Wait," I said out loud, "my God she's following Jody's motorcycle trail." It was a course he and his friends had laid out to practice for moto-cross racing.

Duski never veered from that trail, although it was now almost obscured by overgrowth. It was as if she had been set free. Her ears flapping, feet flying, she jumped and lunged and ran the whole course. She stopped and sat, caught her breath and then ran it again; as Jody often did when he knew he could do it better, faster than before. Out of breath and panting she sat at my feet looking up at me. With her muzzle wide open, her tongue hanging out, she appeared to be smiling. My tears came, but they weren't sad ones.

CHAPTER THREE
The Beach
2001 – The Present

As Jack and I walk the wide Delaware beach, Angel wanders up to the snow fencing that protects the dunes. The scent of other dogs attracts her. Duski used to do the same thing in Ocean City. I'd let her wander, give her the freedom to roam—though not out of sight— while I preferred to walk by the edge of the ocean. It's cooler by the water, and I feel more at peace there watching the waves, the never ending rise and fall of the water, rushing in and sliding back out. For me it has always been reassuring, a repetition of the ages, like the flow of life.

Did I think, back then, that the spirit of my son had come back in the form of little Duski Dog? I did let myself think that, from time to time. It was comforting. But the logical side of me said that it couldn't be. I'd never seriously thought about reincarnation. My Christian upbringing rejected it. I had learned nothing in Sunday school about past lives or next lives, only heaven and hell, after one life. And even if there were a chance that reincarnation could occur, people didn't come back as animals. Did they? It had to be a coincidence that she was so familiar with everything and everyone when she arrived; a fluke that she chose the motorcycle course on which to exercise and play as young dogs do.

And so I didn't talk about the coincidences. I would have felt foolish to do so. I could imagine the thoughts and comments. "Poor Susan, grief has pushed this formerly clear-thinking news reporter over the edge of reality and into the twilight zone. She thinks her dog is her son."

But then there was the time I drove to the Pennsylvania property with Duski in the car. My first husband, John, had bought the wooded parcel that borders the Caledonia State Park. He and several of his friends had each bought one of these lots to use as campsites and to have access to the miles and miles of trails in the mountainous park that could be used legally for motorcycle riding. John had a motor-home, behind which he pulled a trailer capable of hauling five motorcycles. He and Jody and our daughters spent many week-ends and summer vacations camping there and riding the beautiful mountain range. Those were good times for them. I had thought to sell the land after John's death, but Marjorie and Jody, the two most interested in off-road motorcycle riding, asked me if they could keep it. Their sister and I and John's brother, the children's uncle, who was handling the estate, agreed that the two of them should have it. Upon Jody's death, Marjorie took over as the sole proprietor. She rarely uses it but has held onto it as an investment property, or for future use by her family, which includes two boys who also like to ride dirt bikes and 4-wheelers.

I drove there with Duski to check on the lot, a vacant, undeveloped property subject to misuse. I wanted to make sure it hadn't been abused by trespassers, or used as a dumping ground for trash and litter. Neither Marjorie nor I had been there since before Jody's death, perhaps more than a year before. I had the time now and, with Marjorie on the west coast, I thought it was something that needed to be done. But it was also a chance to try and re-connect with the past; to return to a time when my son was alive; a place that knew his laughter, and echoed his heartbeat. A time and place where there had been life, not just memories.

Having only been there once before, I was relieved to find, in the back of the kitchen catch-all drawer, the old map that had once been kept in the glove compartment of the motor-home. Unfolding it, spreading it out on the passenger seat next to me, I smoothed the frayed folds and went over the route. As we drove, Duski slept, without stirring, on the back seat for most of the two-hour trip, that took us out through Gettysburg and into the mountains west of there.

It was when I pulled off the paved highway, and onto the wide dirt road that led through the park to the campsite, that Duski not only moved but became animated. She stood up on her hind legs to look out of the side window. Then she started to whine, a high pitched, pulsating sound that rose to an excited yap. It was unlike her. Duski was a quiet dog, not yappy. She barely barked at all. She jumped across the seat and stood to look out of the other side window. Then she leaped up onto the ledge at the back window to look from there.

The wide, hard packed dirt road led up one side of the mountain, and wound down the other. The directions showed a turn onto a narrower road that led through a stream and then a sharp right turn into the campsite. When I forded the stream Duski jumped and barked frantically. After making the turn into the campsite and stopping, I opened my door and she lunged over me to get out first. Off the dog went, following the trail that, I then remembered, led into the mountain park and the motorcycle trails beyond. I stood motionless. I didn't run after her or try to call her back. I felt an unusual calm, not worrying for a second that she might get lost and not find her way back.

CHAPTER FOUR

I cautiously began sharing those "Duski experiences" with a select few, tempering the telling with a voice of disbelief. I started with Jack. "The strangest thing happened a couple of weeks ago when I was out in the woods with Duski. And you know the day I drove out to the Pennsylvania property? You're not going to believe how she reacted there." Would he, I wondered.

Jack knew how amazed we all were, including his son, that Duski seemed right at home from the first day she arrived. "You think that dog is your son, don't you?" he said with an understanding smile. He was not judgmental or patronizing, but he is much too physicalistic to believe that such a thing could happen.

Jack has always been clear in his beliefs, which reject all spiritual theory as being impossible. He believes that we live, we die, one life and that's it, and that the rewards we reap for good and the punishments for evil are experienced within that one lifetime, or lost forever.

I'd answer Jack with a shrug, and let it go. I wasn't convinced enough to debate the point. But what other explanation could there be?

I hinted with humor at my silly thoughts to the mother of the boy who had been Jody's best friend. "You know," she said, "a big black dog showed up after my first husband's death and I always thought it was him. God—that was one mean dog. It finally got run over by a car and that was that."

My daughter Marjorie believed, but then she believes that every living creature has a spirit or soul, a reason, a predetermined purpose. She thinks that there is no such thing as a chance meeting. That if we are aware and receptive, each life that crosses our path has a message of importance to deliver; that there is no such thing as a coincidence. She also believes in astrology and destiny.

At that time, in the late 1970s, I had just begun my interest in astrology. I had begun to read books on the subject and found myself reading horoscope books with daily predictions for the year.

Jack said then, and would still ask today, "How can all of humanity fit into or be guided by twelve signs?" He has a point, but as I now know, people who delve into astrology have charts drawn up based on the time, date and place of their birth, which takes into consideration the positions of all the major planets at that specific moment, which greatly increases the combination of planetary placements under which someone can be born; going well beyond the twelve zodiac signs.

In all things unscientific there are perhaps more questions than answers, with a lot of supposing. Suppose this little dog was my son reincarnated. Why did he return and in that form?

Most people, who believe in reincarnation, believe that the one thing that a soul carries with it, from one lifetime to the next, is its karma.

Karma is described as "cause and effect." Karma means action. The acts we commit have consequence; everything we do, the good as well as the bad, shapes and creates our destiny.

Reincarnation is an intricate part of the Buddhist and Hindu religions. And they believe that the lessons and experiences of each lifetime create our karma. Non-virtuous acts must be atoned for or changed in this life or carried over into the next—just as virtuous deeds, that may not be rewarded in this life, can be carried over into the next in an effort to achieve a totally enlightened or virtuous state known as nirvana.

It is believed that what we are now is based on conditions of our past, and that what we become in the future will be affected by what we do in the present.

Examples of the cause and effect of karma might be: A life of lying could lead to a future life where people speak untruthfully about you or deceive you. A life of stealing could lead to a new life of poverty. Sexual misconduct, such as adultery, could result in future lives in which your companions would be unfaithful or untrustworthy.

If Duski carried Jody's soul, what karma did his soul bring with it?

The act of killing, taking a life, even one's own life, affects not only the victim but those who love and depend on that person as well. There are consequences of suicide, beyond the death of one person.

Jody was also obsessed with his girlfriend. His suicide note read: "I loved her too much." the Buddhist would describe Jody's feelings as more of an extreme attachment than pure love. Although many animals form lifelong relationships, they are not obsessive.

Jody was a shy teenager who couldn't find a way to talk about the pain and problems in his life. He never experienced the relief and resolution of verbalizing his feelings in order to successfully handle them. Dogs have other ways of communicating and dealing with feelings; reacting and responding on a more immediate, open basis, whether it pertains to other animals or the humans in their lives.

On the positive side: Jody was a devoted son. His love for me, and for all of his family, never faltered. His love for me was as pure as a love could be, with thoughtful devotion and kindness that spanned his years from early childhood to the time of his death at seventeen. But the security of the love he needed in return was shattered by divorce and his father's suicide. He never experienced the comfort of believing that his family would always be there.

If Duski carried Jody's spirit and karma, would Jody's unconditional love be rewarded in Duski's life and would Jody's desire for a close family be achieved by the little dog that was living his next life?

CHAPTER FIVE

California

Summer 1978

Even at low tide the waves break hard against the large boulders jutting out of the sand; their spray tossed high against the backdrop of the setting sun, defusing the vivid shades of orange and gold. The water rushes in between and around the rock statuary on the northern California coast, forming tidal pools when the ocean recedes.

I pick Duski up in my arms, carrying her, as I wade through the pools to the other side where the beach is wide and long. The Pacific coast beaches are so different from the ones at home in the east. I'm awed by the cliffs that drop to the sea. And the sand is coarser, the color of stone and rock rather than shells.

We've come to California to visit Marjorie, her fiancé and Jackson, the Doberman Pincher. They found a place that's both charming and affordable, a hard combination to locate in San Francisco. Jack and Christopher, Duski and I have made the trip but O'Donnell is spending the summer as a counselor at a camp in North Carolina, where she spent many wonderful summers as a camper.

It should be a good time for us but it's not. It is good to see the kids and how they're carving out a new life for themselves. My future son-in-law, a singer, guitarist and composer, has established the band he's always wanted, and the band is enjoying a fair degree of success in the northern California region. Duski and Jackson seem happy to have reconnected and romp playfully in a park near the apartment on Jackson Street. But it's not a good time for Jack and me.

It's been a year since Jody's death, a year of struggling with my feelings and emotions; trying to sort out the grief and the guilt, trying desperately to hold on to the love I feel for Jack, but not sure I can. I often feel too drained to deal with "us." It sometimes seems easier to walk away. A void might bring safety, at least numbness. And I fear the responsibility—the pressure—of keeping him happy. What becomes of him if I fail? I'm barely surviving myself.

I pull him close and try to forget—to build something new on the old shaken foundation, but not really believing in the strength of what we had—before all the sadness.

So I push him away, not feeling certain enough of myself to shore us up.

It's no good for either of us. Jack's been patient and understanding, hoping we could and would return to what we had for two years before Jody's death, the family we had become, without the formality of marriage. It had been good. Jody, and O'Donnell and Marjorie, when she was home, the siblings Christopher always wanted. He looked up to Jody and his friends. He and Jack went to Jody's motorcycle races. Christopher and O'Donnell romped and kidded with each other. There had been a lot of laughter in the house; Christmases to cherish, summer vacations at the beach.

But not now. I'm building an emotional wall between Jack and me. We've argued on this trip, and it hasn't been pleasant. Marjorie doesn't want to be caught in the middle, in a position of counseling or choosing sides. She went through that when her father and I were divorcing—she doesn't want to do it again and she says so. She's right—she's got her own issues to sort out in the wake of her father's and brother's deaths.

Jack and I decide to make a break, right here in California, in the middle of our vacation. He's taken Christopher down to Los Angeles to visit Disneyland. Duski and I are touring the coast from Carmel down to Big Sur. We'll go back to San Francisco to fly home; they'll return from L.A.

Duski is such a comfort. I hold her as I sit on the beach and watch the sun go down. She licks my tears away. I talk to her, I share my deepest thoughts and fears. I wish she could help me make some sense of this separation I've imposed. I look into those knowing eyes, so strong, yet sensitive and resolute. I feel reassured, calmer, stronger to face whatever lies ahead.

A bird skitters across the beach at the edge of the ocean. It looks like a sandpiper, but it's bigger than I'm used to seeing on the east coast, and redder. Tensing, Duski lunges off my lap and chases after it, but it's she who gets caught, by a wave rolling on shore. Her short little legs and low belly are soaked and she scurries away, out of reach, farther back on the beach where it's dry, now forgetting about the bird. She shakes off the water and tip-toes back toward me. Shaking each foot as she lifts it, as if to drip dry her legs on the way back. It makes me smile. She is definitely not a water dog.

Watching her I'm reminded of Jody when he was a little boy at the beach. He was also timid about getting wet. He didn't rush gleeful or carefree into the ocean, as some kids do, to the worry of their parents. I'd hold his hand and we'd stand at the edge of the dry sand and let the waves slowly come to us. He'd barely allow his toes to get wet before backing away. Eventually he'd let me carry him in, and hold him in waist deep water. With his legs wrapped tightly around my hips I'd hold him firmly; jumping up with each wave so that it wouldn't splash his face.

When he did learn to swim it was a struggle for that reason. Putting his face in the water brought on panic. It took the good natured persuasion of a 17-year-old lifeguard at the nearby swim club we joined for a couple of years. Todd didn't embarrass Jody, or shame him into going underwater, but kidded with him and made it fun, while establishing a goal. He told Jody that when he could swim the length of the pool with his face in the water it would earn him the right to swim in the deep end with his sisters and the other older children. When the challenge was met I'm not sure who was prouder of the accomplishment, Jody or the patient teenage teacher.

After that, Jody had more fun in the water. He was never a great swimmer, but he became comfortable enough to flip off the diving board and enjoy himself with other kids his age. It helped that when he was ten years old we put in a backyard pool and he was able to swim more often. At the end, last summer, vacationing in Ocean City, he was riding really big waves with his friends—too big—I thought and it was then I who was worried and apprehensive about the danger of what he was doing.

"Just a year ago," I think with sadness, "everything was so different just one year ago." I feel the heat of tears burning my eyes and following a familiar path down my cheeks.

At home, back at work, Jack and I go about our jobs; not exactly avoiding each other, but skirting opportunities to be alone. It's not all that hard to do in the hectic, deadline driven TV news business, where most of the time we're out working on separate stories in separate locations and the rest of the time we're focused on getting our individual daily report on the air, on time. Part of the change, for me, is leaving for home as soon as I'm off the air; not unwinding with my co-workers, including Jack, by rehashing the day's efforts—the rewards as well as the missed opportunities—or comparing how we covered a story with our competitors, at other stations. It's actually an important part of broadcast news and was one of the most enjoyable parts of my day with Jack. We're both miserable.

Two weeks go by, Jack calls to ask if he can come out to the house. "I just want to talk—I want you to understand some things." I feel pressure, not sure of my resolve. But, I would like to see him away from the job, so I agree.

Duski greets him excitedly, then sits up on her hind legs and begs, the way he taught her to do when she wanted something. I smile, there is no doubt what she wants now.

We go out on the porch, all three of us. When we sit down, Duski jumps up into my lap. Jack looks at me intently, with tenderness; leaning over, he pets Duski as he kisses me gently.

"I've missed you," he says softly.

"I've missed you too," I swallow to control the emotion.

"Look," he begins, taking my hand in his, "I love you, you know that." I nod. "More than any woman I've ever known. I would like to be a part of your life—for as long as I'm allowed, by you," he shrugs, "or some greater power." He smiles, I laugh. "But if you decide you don't love me, or simply decide you don't want to share your life with me—for whatever reason, I'll be okay. I'll go on working, I'll have my life with my son, I'll even date other women. I'll be fine. I'd rather go on loving you, seeing you, having a life with you, but if you choose not to let that happen, my life will not end.

"But even if I lose your love, I don't want to lose your friendship. It's ridiculous for us to go on being cool to each other at work. If you don't love me it's okay, but I'm still your friend."

The understanding of what he has said comes quickly. The reaction is slow and warm, and envelopes me. My heart seems to expand; my lungs fill up and I'm breathing with ease. My pulse races but I feel calm.

Holding tightly the dog in my lap, feeling her heart beating wildly, I pull her close.

I am free. Free to love without it being a matter of life and death. Jack has set me free. I don't have to love him—but I'm free to do so, without life threatening consequences, and so I do—with all my heart.

A year later we're married on the south lawn outside the farm house. The late afternoon sun filters through a yellow and white striped tent, turning everything under it to gold. Our friends and colleagues attend, Marjorie and O'Donnell are my maids-of-honor. Jack's son, at age 8, is his best man. Sitting at our feet, as we say our vows, is Duski Dog.

CHAPTER SIX
The Farm
2001

The new kitchen is so spacious and so much more inviting. Elegant is the one word that Jack and I keep using to describe it. From the Italian tile floor, dark cherry cabinets and open space it's so different from our old one, built hastily after the house fire in 1979.

The fire occurred during a violent thunderstorm two months after our wedding. Neither of us was home at the time, but Duski was, along with her seven two-week-old puppies. Duski had fallen for a hound dog from the neighboring farm, and without our knowledge or consent had given in to the passion. But as with most unplanned, or even unwanted pregnancies, as mine was with Jody, when Duski's off-spring arrived we were thrilled and enchanted and instantly in love.

The night that the puppies were born, Jack and I stayed up very late with Duski, watching and helping as the perfectly formed, wiggly, whimpering little creatures made their way into this world. Duski would clean each one upon its arrival, licking away the moisture of birth. With their eyes sealed shut, the puppies moved instinctively to position themselves for their first meal.

We watched, and toasted with wine, this miracle of nature and new life. Jack had opened a good bottle of red wine—as he does on all special occasions: Christmas and New Year's Eve; pay day; a snow storm; the melting of snow; a sunny day or rain, almost every day presents an excuse to taste a good wine. (Jack has now reached the age and stage where excuses aren't needed, just reaching another day is reason enough to celebrate.) "So much good wine, so little time."

Duski was a devoted and constantly caring mother; proud as well. She showed off her pups to all who came to visit. We had Duski, and her brood, bedded down in the mud room/laundry room just inside the back door. The tile floor made cleanups easy and the doorway to the kitchen could be closed off with a baby gate at bedtime, and when we were at work.

On evenings, and week-ends, when we were home, we left the doorway open to the kitchen, and the rest of the house, so that Duski didn't feel isolated and cut off from her human family. And when visitors were there, if they didn't go in to where the puppies were, Duski would bring them into the living room, one at a time, by the scruff of their necks, to be inspected and praised.

With their mixed heritage each one of the pups was different; no two looked anything alike. It was fun to guess what they might look like when they were grown. They all had satin smooth coats, unlike the wildly wiry coat of their mother. Some were brown and white, like their father, some were black, some were a combination. A big brown male, the strongest and most active, commanded and got the most attention, from his mother and visitors alike. Christopher labeled that one his. There was a sleek black female, with a slash of white on her chest and two white paws. She had a classic head and if it weren't for the white, she would have resembled a miniature black lab. They were all beautiful, perfectly formed, and kept impeccably clean by Duski's constant grooming.

On the evening of the fire, Jack was anchoring the newscast and I was reporting "live" from the Inner Harbor. My mother and father, then living in their home on the same property—the house Marjorie now owns—would later tell us that a severe storm, with the worst lightning to hit the area in more than a decade, passed directly over our house between 5:30 and 6:30 p.m.

When the thunder and lightning passed, and the downpour subsided, my mother, looking from her front window, saw what she thought was mist lifting up off the hot steamy, rain soaked earth behind our house. It rose slowly, but did not clear even when the sun came out. In fact it thickened. "I think Susie's house is on fire," she said with alarm to my father. My father went to check and found flames spewing from the rear windows of the first floor and quickly called the local volunteer fire company.

In the newsroom, just off the air, Jack got what he thought, at first, was a crank call. A female voice that did not identify herself said, "Your house is on fire, everything's gone." But, then she added, "I think the dogs got out, I'm not sure, but everything else is gone." Jack then recognized the voice of my mother, in an excited and confused state of panic.

Thinking that the house and its contents were destroyed and that to hurry would serve no purpose, Jack picked up Christopher as planned and together they drove to the farm. Trying to remain as calm as possible, Jack talked to his son about what had happened, to prepare him for the devastating sight that awaited them.

I, on the other hand, left my live location knowing nothing. Anxious to get off from work that day, to spend a lovely summer evening with my new husband and stepson, as soon as my report was over, I got in my car and left for home. Since it was before the age of cell phones, when Jack got off the air and learned the news, he was unable to reach me and warn me about what had happened to our house.

I stopped at the grocery store to shop for dinner, even buying a bottle of wine I thought he'd like. My spirits were high as I drove over the Liberty Reservoir bridge, winding up through the pines.

The trees sparkled as the setting sun shone through the droplets of rain still clinging to the branches. I was singing along happily with a song on the radio as I crested the last hill before reaching the road that leads to our farm.

Stunned by the sight of fire trucks lining the small country road, I pulled to the shoulder and got out quickly. I saw no fire. Thinking more like a reporter than an area resident I ran to a neighbor standing in the middle of the road.

"What's going on? What's happening? Where's the fire?"

He searched my face before responding.

"Don't you know?" He could see I didn't. "It's your house."

My hand covered my mouth in shock. My eyes, so accustomed to tears, burned anew as my gaze searched the horizon at the end of the long road and dirt driveway into the farm. Smoke funneled into the sky and the realization of truth hit me. Barely able to walk, my vision blurred, I staggered in the direction of my home. As I started up the dirt driveway I saw someone coming down. A dark image against a smoke-filled sky. It was Jack. We stumbled into each other's arms. "I can't take anymore," I choked out. "I can't. This is it. I can't go on—I just don't have the strength to begin again."

Jack gently brushed the tears from my face and pulled me back into his arms. He held me very, very tight and his words were soft next to my ear. "Look, your things from your former life have burned, and mine from my former life have burned. Now we'll build ours."

I knew in that moment, with those words, that I could go on. I knew I would do whatever it took to continue a life with this man whose love would see me through. It wouldn't be easy, life rarely is, but it would be worth the struggle.

As we walked up the hill to the burned-out house, Jack prepared me for what I would find. My mother had been wrong, had jumped to conclusions. The house was not completely destroyed. Somehow, the quick action of four volunteer fire companies had saved the old frame structure.

The fire had started in the kitchen, lightning coming in through a TV set that had been sitting on the kitchen counter and fanned out from there. Most of the downstairs was gutted; the rest suffered only smoke damage.

"Duski?" I almost screamed it out. "What about Duski?"

CHAPTER SEVEN
The Farm
August 1979

---

*F*ire trucks block the driveway, sit angled on every side of the house. Hoses crisscross the lawn, lights flash. The smell of smoke is so heavy in the hot humid air it seems hard to breathe. Or perhaps it's because my heart, pounding so hard, seems caught in my throat. I try swallowing to make it calm. As a reporter I've covered many house fires. Now I understand the helpless despair on the faces of those victims. The back of the house is charred black, the windows are broken and burned out. The back door is gone.

"I've looked all around the house and the barn," Jack says, "but I can't find her." Adding quickly in an effort to try and reassure me, "Your mother says she got out. The firemen found two of the puppies outside the door and a neighbor took them to the vet."

I stare at the black hole where the backdoor used to be. That morning we had left the door ajar so that Duski could get in and out as she needed to, never imagining she'd need to escape from a fire.

Jack is trying to be calm—trying to keep me calm. "She got two puppies out. The firemen said one of the puppies was singed, so the flames must have been pretty intense in there." He motions with his hand. "Duski's too smart to run back into a wall of fire like that."

"Singed," I say aloud, horrified at the scene I envision. My eyes fixed on the burned-out door, I can almost feel the heat, sense the panic Duski must have felt as she struggled to save her babies. She must have gone back in when the house was fully engulfed; burning out of control, flames so hot and low that they would singe a puppy on the floor. She couldn't have gotten under the flames, she had to go through them. Did her fur catch on fire as well? How many times did she try; challenging the inferno; unable to breathe; smoke searing her eyes. What was she thinking, feeling? The anguish of seeing those new little lives that she had given life and love to—dying. Powerless to stop it from happening. Her will, determination and courage, not enough. Eventually having to turn away, and let them burn.

I spin around. "Duski," I begin screaming. "Duski—come here. Please!" I beg—"please, please come here." I stumble out into the darkness, away from the blaring lights and noise of the two-way radios coming from the emergency vehicles.

Jack walks the other way also shouting her name. On the other side of the paddock fence, standing inside the barnyard, I scan the pasture calling her name. I see movement in the tall grass coming up from the woods. "Duski, come here girl—come on—it's all right—I'm home." I drop to my knees, and stretch out my hands to pull her in. "Thank God," I whisper, "Thank God you're all right." She's trembling, whimpering, her coat is damp and reeks of smoke, but she's not burned. I bury my face in the pungent fur and weep, for her pain and mine.

Calling out to Jack that I've found our dog I hurry back to take her over to my mother and father's house where we'll be staying, for however long, until we can rent something, perhaps in town, closer to work. I try to move my thoughts away, back to Duski. I'm not ready to think about the weeks and months ahead, and what it will take to clean up and rebuild. Maybe we won't rebuild. Maybe it's time to move on? Maybe we should start over somewhere else—so much pain here—too much maybe? "Don't," I say out loud. "Not now."

I hold Duski tightly in my arms as Jack and I make our way around the smoldering debris at the back of the house. Duski struggles to break free. Tightening my grip I look at Jack. "The puppies," I mouth. She struggles harder, but can't wiggle out of my firm hold. I bend my head close to hers. "I know you got two of them out," I say softly, as if she can understand. "They've been taken to the vet—maybe you'll see them tomorrow." I hug her close.

But there will be no tomorrow for the pups. We get a call and are told that they died—heat and smoke inhalation.

The night is a long, restless one. Duski keeps jumping off our bed and going to the front door, whining to get out. I pick her up and carry her back. "Not yet," I tell her gently, "we'll go out in the morning, when it's light."

At dawn I feel exhausted. This time, with Jack by my side, I open the door and she starts to run for our home. "No," I yell as I take off after her, dressed only in the nightgown I borrowed from my mother. The morning dew is cold on my bare feet as I run down the grassy bank and through the garden between the two houses. "Come back Duski! You shouldn't go over there."

Jack catches up to me as I round the corner of the house, and there near the back steps to the burned-out backdoor is Duski, digging frantically under a log. We walk to her and watch as a shallow bunker of dirt is uncovered and a whimpering black puppy is carefully lifted out by its mother's mouth. It's the shiny black female with the white chest and paws. Holding the puppy by the back of its neck, Duski shakes it gently to remove the dirt and carries it to my waiting hands. I look up at Jack, who is as stunned as I.

Duski had apparently gotten three puppies out before the flames and heat became too intense to go back in, and this one she had been able to cover with a protective shield of dirt, with space to breathe. "How did she know to do that?" I question, as I watch her search for the others.

Jack moves closer and gently strokes the cold, hungry, but uninjured puppy I'm cuddling in my hands. We watch as Duski thoroughly searches the area where she last saw the other two she had gotten out. Not finding them, she enters the ruins of the room where the remainder of her brood had been. One by one she brings the charred bodies to the bottom of the steps. One by one the cold, lifeless, blackened forms are lined up until there are four.

"That's it Duski," I choke out. "That's all there are." She licks each of the puppies as if to make sure there is no life, or perhaps to say good-bye.

Jack looks at me, his eyes rimmed with tears. I stoop down and pick up Duski, holding her with the squirming puppy, that is so glad to be back with its mother. I carry Duski because I know she won't go on her own. "Let's go to the other house, let's show everyone else the puppy you've saved."

I'll come back to bury the others, and I know I'll have to get the bodies of the other two from the vet and let Duski see them, because I know that there will be no peace for her until she knows what happened to each one of her babies. We name the lone survivor Blaze.

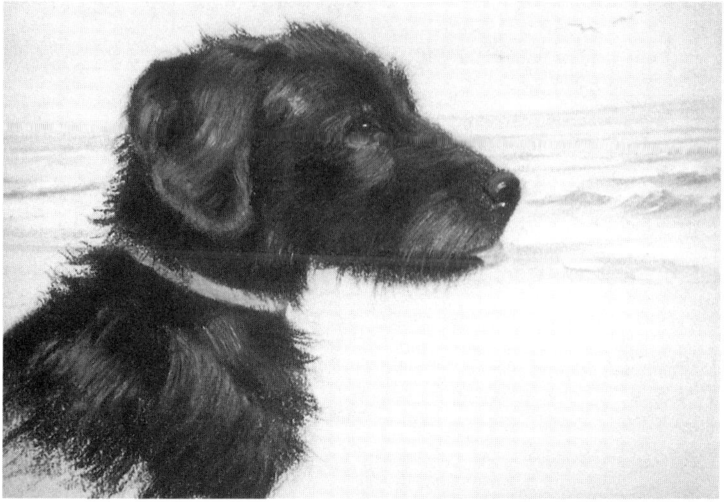

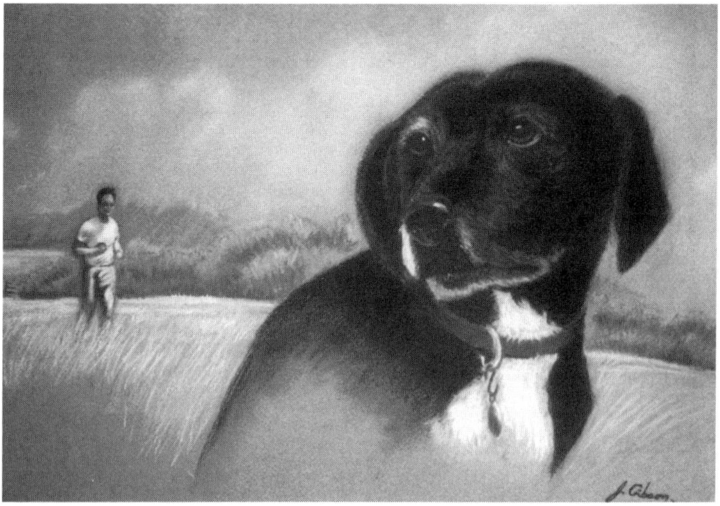

CHAPTER EIGHT
The Apartment
1980

It takes less than five minutes to drive from the TV station to the apartment. It's too close. One of the things I liked about living on the farm, 45 minutes away from my work, was that it gave me time to unwind, to mull over the day and then put it behind me.

Routinely, by the time I crossed the bridge over the Liberty Reservoir going into Carroll County, I'd feel the stress and pressures of the day ebb to the back of my mind. It was as if there were an imaginary toll booth, a depository demanding the worries of the job before allowing me to continue on my way. Now, there is no time to let go, and the problems and disappointments of the day go with me, adding to whatever challenges might await me at home. Referring to the apartment as home seems jarring, an inappropriate description of what it means to us. A dwelling, residence, living quarters, all would better describe our view of it. But for now it's the only home we have. At least, I still have Duski riding with me. She is a calming influence, although from her perspective the ride is also too short. Just when she gets settled in, we've arrived at the apartment and it's time to get out of the car.

I turn the key in the front door lock of the spacious 3rd-floor walk-up apartment with two large bedrooms, two baths, kitchen, dining room, large living room, and outdoor balcony. But it's sparsely furnished with cheap looking, rented furniture and I hate it.

Duski rushes past me as I open the door; anxious to check on her puppy, Blaze, now seven months old. Duski has become a devoted mother to her only remaining offspring, barking reprimands when the puppy ventures into risky situations, and licking her with affection when Blaze responds properly. Duski has also taught by example—for instance Blaze became housebroken almost immediately, always following her mother outside. Duski has become her daughter's best friend, always willing to frolic with her, and in their mock fights letting Blaze seem to win. The racing and rolling around with her mother has help to burn off some of Blaze's youthful energy. But not all of it. And though house trained, Blaze has been creating another kind of mess, brought about by that youthful energy, curiosity, and her unfair confinement, necessitated by apartment living.

I can't take Blaze in the car with Duski everyday, because she'd tear the car apart, since she is also at the height of the chewing stage. So we confine Blaze to either the powder room, or, if it's warm outside, we leave her closed out on the balcony.

So far, Blaze has occupied her days by pulling strips of wallpaper off the bathroom walls, unrolling the toilet paper, pulling the towels off the racks and shedding the shower curtain.

Out on the balcony she has pulled up the indoor/outdoor carpet from both ends. Our security deposit has long since been spent and now we're working on what else we will owe. I'm sure Duski, as well as I, wonders what mess we will find today.

With my hand on the door knob of the powder room I pause, take a deep breath and prepare myself for what I might find. Duski looks up at me as if to say, "Patience—remember whatever you find be patient—she's just a puppy. My puppy!" Jack and I both have experienced lapses in calm when greeted with some of Blaze's acts of destructive puppy behavior. The reprimands have been closely watched by Duski and if judged too stern she steps in to distract us in some cunning, cute way; sitting up and begging, jumping up on the sofa and burying her head under a pillow or going to the front door and scratching to get out.

I slowly open the door and Blaze rushes out. She is so glad to see us. "Hello—girl—how are you?" I pet her head and rub her back with both hands. She wiggles her approval. As I go on patting her, showing my affection, I peer over her into the bathroom. It looks okay. The throw rug is matted down where she's been sleeping—but other than that there is no sign of her boring day.

"Good Girl! Good Blaze Starski," my pet name for her; patterned after the famous Baltimore stripper, and the "ski" part of her mother's name.

Duski jumps up and licks my face. She likes it when everyone in the family is getting along.

It's been hard on us all, these past months. There has been a lot of tension. I've never been called thin, but now I am; usually a good thing when you're on television, but this isn't good. Living in this apartment, I've often felt as Blaze must, confined to a restrictive environment without knowing exactly when it will end. And we spend every weekend trying to get the house back together. The dogs like going to the farm every Saturday and Sunday, where they can run free without any restrictions, but it's not a pastime I'd recommend for most newlyweds, as I have to keep reminding myself that Jack and I are.

First, there was cleaning up, and sorting through all the charred remains to get an accounting for the insurance company. Now, we do what we can to help the workmen and to clean up the yard. I don't think we'll ever get all the broken glass picked up.

The good part has been the workmen—most of them neighbors. They came in a group, when they heard that we were greatly under insured, and that I was thinking about not rebuilding. There was a 70-year-old retired carpenter, an electrician, a brick mason and several strong young men who could do almost anything, and they all wanted to help.

They stood at what used to be the back door, and one of them said, "When do you want us to get started? If we start right away there's a good chance you'll be back home in less than a year." I was touched, and told them so, but I was not yet sure we should rebuild. At that point Jack and I hadn't talked it through. I had prepared arguments in favor of leaving, arguments that had been seeded by a friend.

"You really should leave this house," she said. "Look at all the bad things that have happened here—your ex-husband—your son—now this fire. You have a chance to get away—you should do it. You owe it to Jack—you owe it to yourself, for that matter, you owe it to your marriage. What chance do you think it has of surviving with all this baggage challenging you both every day."

"Yes, I thought, "she's probably right." We probably would be better off starting over somewhere else. The house was under insured—for just sixty thousand dollars, including structure and contents. (You never think something like a house fire is going to happen to you.) But $60,000 would be a good down payment on a very nice house somewhere else. We could bulldoze this house, take the money and start over, without all the work of cleaning up and rebuilding.

Jack had other ideas. "I love it here. I love the country," he said. That coming from a man who had lived most of his life in the city. "I love the open space—I love the location, here on the reservoir. Where are you ever going to find another property that comes close to the advantages of this one. Besides, you can't run away. Do you think if you moved to California you'd forget that your son committed suicide? What your ex-husband did; what Jody did—for whatever reason—was not the result of some evil power hiding in the walls of this house. Those tragedies cannot be blamed on this house.

"And what about all the good things that have happened in this house? The three children, including your son, you raised here—the first steps they took on these floors—the birthday parties and Christmases."

I think about what Jack is saying, and search for the images to go with the memories that span more than twenty years. They're all there, tucked away in my mind, in the various forms and phases of a growing family. The young daughters, Marjorie and O'Donnell, figuring out their fit within the family and the house, while searching for their individual identities. I can see the quizzical look on two-year-old Marjorie's face when we brought her baby sister home from the hospital, putting the baby in a crib in the room that had been Marjorie's alone. "Is this really necessary," she seemed to be saying. It was necessary for many years, because at first there were only two bedrooms in the yet unfinished house.

And then when I became pregnant with Jody we built a wing onto the house which gave us three bedrooms; my husband John and mine, the girls' and Jody's. But the sisters were so different that when they approached the pre-teen years we realized that if we didn't separate them there would be no peace in the house for any of us. That's when we moved Jody to the third floor.

Using inexpensive walnut paneling the attic space was quickly walled in. The built-in chest of drawers, and thick carpet on the floor and stairs made it very comfortable, even cozy. John did all the work, and Jody helped, which gave them time together as father and son with a common goal. When it was finished and Jody moved in, he seemed delighted to have his own more masculine space, apart from the girls, on a separate floor. I guess it was almost like a boys' club house or tree house with privacy rules on who could come in.

The endless images created over the years by the dozens of those special occasions Jack referred to, such as birthdays and Christmases, come back to me in a barrage of snapshots. I see the girls and their friends seated around the dining room table, acting like grownups. They are all dressed up in party clothes, heads full of curls and ribbons, faces aglow as they blow out the candles on the cake. In one picture it's Marjorie's birthday and she's at the head of the table. In another it's O'Donnell's and she's seated up there. Jody is there too; as a baby, a toddler; a little boy with light blonde hair and there is always a smile. On one of his birthdays I see him in the kitchen. There's chocolate all over his face. He's helping me make the cake for his party.

My mind moves forward ten years and Jody is in an upstairs bedroom. It's 1975, January or February. Jody is not yet fifteen. His dad has only been dead a couple of months. Jody is taking over as the man of the house, or that's what it seems he's trying to do. Marjorie's in Africa and he's helping me to paint her room for when she returns. The room had been a soft pink, but this is the era of psychedelic colors and I've chosen something I think is more "with it." The paint chip is labeled "Hot Hot Salmon," and I think that should be cool. Jody is not so sure. The paint looks almost a reddish/orange as we start putting it on. With each brush stroke Jody stares, at the paint and then me. Finally he stops. "Do you really think she's going to like this?" he asks, knowing that she won't.

"It's not too bad," I say, trying to reassure him that we're not wasting out time. "It's just wet. It'll look better, softer, when it drys."

Of course it didn't, and Jody begged me to get some other paint, saying that he'd redo it by himself. I said we should wait to see what Marjorie said. Of course she hated it and then Jody helped her repaint it, all the while complaining that he could have had it done before she got home, if I'd just listened to him.

And now, I think, those walls are blackened, covered with soot and smoke damage and will have to be repainted again. But, I stop in mid-thought realizing that underneath the coat of black, and the top coat of paint, is that hideous color that Jody and I put on together. And my mind is flooded with every detail and memory and feeling of that day. How we joked and laughed, seemingly wasting our time creating such an ugly room. How we giggled, the two of us, imagining just what Marjorie's reaction would be. There had been months without even smiles and now we laughed and it felt so good.

In the rubble of destruction there are sounds, and feelings, and hope, however faint at times, of what can be again if you don't walk away.

Jack is continuing to convince, although I no longer need to be swayed.

"We are born and we die—but in between there is living—and I would very much like to live here. If you want to talk about fate, and acts of God, maybe the fire was such an act, and now we do have an opportunity to build our home, yours and mine, in this house.

I look at Duski and her pleading eyes. The fire caused her much more pain than it did me, and she seems to want to come home. We all agree that we will stay.

CHAPTER NINE
The Farm
November 2001 – The Present

"The dance floor should go here," Marjorie says with a sweeping gesture of her hand. Then, running to the other side of the lawn, "the food stations here," turning, gesturing and pacing, "and the chairs set up here in two sections, with an aisle in the middle facing the arbor. The wedding cake right here in the middle." She pauses—"But, maybe the dance floor and band should be over here instead and the food stations over there."

While Marjorie's fiancé, Todd Laudeman, and I watch, along with the man representing the tent rental company, my daughter changes her mind, and the placement of what will be housed under the tent for their wedding about half a dozen times. Marjorie is someone who loves to rearrange the furniture in her house. Todd warns that the items for the wedding are "virtual furniture" that can be moved more easily and thus more often. We all laugh. Finally, when the dance floor is back where it started, Todd says, "I'm going to get a beer." The tent man says, "Can I come with you?" We laugh again. We are having a wonderful time planning for this wedding—set for November 17th.

Todd, 53, eight years older than Marjorie, has been a friend of the family for thirty-five years; though for much of that time the friendship was maintained from a distance. We first met at the nearby swim club where we once belonged. Todd was the 17-year-old life guard who taught Jody to put his face in the water and swim the length of the pool. For the past twenty years, he has lived and worked in New York state, where he owns a home.

It wasn't until the spring of 2000, when his previous marriage had broken up, and Marjorie's divorce from her first husband had become final, that the two reconnected and fell in love. It has been a joy for me to see their two families merge. Todd has two teenaged daughters, Marjorie two teenaged sons. They all get along.

So in love are Marjorie and Todd that I told her one day that I could now die happy. "Don't rush that," she said, "we have a wedding to plan." Marjorie didn't have a big wedding before; she was married in a court house in California. Not this time.

It's been a wedding year. Jack's son Christopher, now 31 was married this past June to a lovely young woman, Melissa MacKinnon, whom he met when they both worked in Washington, D.C. They now live in California, where they share similar professions in the field of internet sales and marketing. The wedding took place in Cape Cod, where her family has roots, a summer home and childhood vacation memories.

Their wedding day was a rare cloudless Cape Cod day, the ceremony outside overlooking the water. Jack stood beside his son, serving as his best man, just as Christopher had been best man for his father at our wedding twenty-two years ago, here on the farm.

The reason I speak of weddings is because it was on my daughter O'Donnell's wedding day that Duski gave me another reason to pause and wonder about her origin. In August of 1981, two years after Jack and I were married, O'Donnell and Steve Timchula were wed, at a lovely church service, with the reception also being held here on the farm. That was about a year after we had moved back into our reconstructed house, after the fire, so it too was a big occasion with many reasons to celebrate.

O'Donnell was a beautiful bride, exceptionally so. Her blonde shoulder-length hair swung loose, swirling back over the lace veil that covered the top of her head, framed her face, and flowed down the back of her gown, extending into a ten foot train. Her ivory gown, with its sweetheart neck, tapered to a narrow waist; the skirt falling softly to the floor with satin and lace.

The professional photographer we'd hired was posing O'Donnell on the south lawn; setting up what was to be a portrait of the bride alone. The sun was soft on her face, the grass and surrounding trees, a deep summer green.

He carefully swirled the long train around in front of her feet. It was the final touch for this elegant picture. He then stepped back behind the camera to set the focus.

At that moment, Duski leaped into the center of the carefully placed train. She did so gingerly, as if not to mess up or soil the perfectly arranged garment. Turning directly to the camera the little dog sat up begging, her front paws held high. O'Donnell laughed, as did those of us watching; then holding our breath we all waited for the shutter to click and the flash to go off.

Instead, the photographer, looking through the lens, saw an intruder; springing out from behind the camera he shooed the dog away before realizing that he had just destroyed the best picture of the day, one that we would have cherished above all the rest.

The image haunted me. Why had Duski done that? She had sat very still, several minutes—until she was shooed away—long enough for even an amateur photographer to get a good shot. Who knows how long she would have stayed there if she hadn't been chased. The perception that stays with me: Duski posing for a family picture on his sister's wedding day.

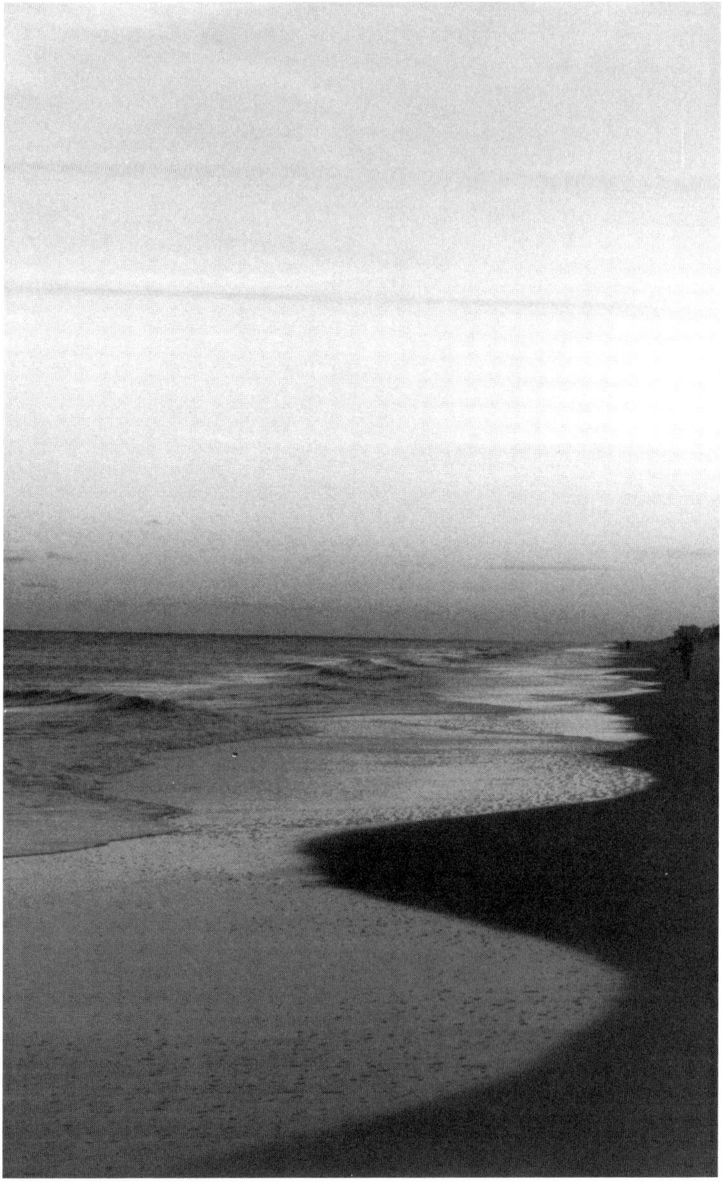

CHAPTER TEN

The Beach

November 30, 2001

The sun setting to the west over Rehoboth Bay illuminates the clouds with a lining of iridescent pink. Turning to the east, a full moon is lifting out of the ocean. It is the second full moon in this month of November and it is even more spectacular than the one before.

We're back at the beach after a beautiful and successful wedding. The November 17th weather was so warm and sunny that, at the last minute and to no one's surprise, Marjorie decided to rearrange the chairs; putting them outside on the front lawn facing the decorated wedding arbor that served as the entrance to the tent. It was the right thing to do and provided, in the middle of November, an extraordinarily lovely outdoor setting for the marriage ceremony.

However, the real warmth of the day was generated by the aura of genuine love and affection coming from the bride and groom for each other and their friends and family. I heard someone say, "There is such positive karma surrounding us here."

Among the guests were some former colleagues who had stood with Marjorie, Jack and me, almost twenty-five years ago, in the hallway of the University of Maryland Shock Trauma Center, as Jody's life was ending. In an effort organized by our News Director, Charlie Horich, after Jody died, they all emptied their pockets of the money they had with them; bills and change, to send the minister, Philip Roulette, who was also there, to Boston where O'Donnell was at college, to tell her what had happened to her brother and to bring her home. We didn't want her to be alone when she got the terrible news. Seeing our pain, these wonderful people had helped and comforted us then. Now, with Marjorie's wedding, they could share our joy.

I have learned to savor these good times, and to relish the quite times, such as we experience here at the beach, off-season. The beach time also provides an opportunity for reflection. Usually, especially when we're young, we're so busy living our lives that there is no time to think about the significance of each day, or even each decade.

Thinking about it now, as I tell this story of Duski, I'm aware that she shared what will probably be the most productive decade of my life. The 1980's brought dramatic change both personally and professionally and that little dog was always there to cheer, console, or share a celebration.

Jack and I co-anchored a top rated newscast during that decade. Christopher would get weary of our shop talk at dinner, but Duski didn't seem to, except when she was sitting up begging for food.

We went out on strike, along with eighteen of our on-air colleagues, to save the right of the American Federation of Television and Radio Artists' union to go on representing us at WMAR-TV, Channel 2. Duski walked the picket line with us for seven weeks and comforted us, despite our fears that we would lose our jobs. We didn't.

My mother and father both died during the 80s. Duski sat by the grave site for services.

It was that decade in which my daughters gave birth to our six grandchildren. Duski welcomed them all and became a tolerant, lovable, patient, real-life stuffed animal that was poked, prodded, pulled and slept upon. As the grandchildren grew, the games changed but Duski was always ready to play.

On snowy days she raced sleds to the bottom of the pasture hills. Her now adult daughter, Blaze, who usually followed Duski everywhere, and was devoted to our family, didn't possess the endurance or the endless desire to participate in the children's play. Duski never tired of the challenge of the chase, and while Blaze would sit at the top

Returning

of the hill and watch, Duski, like the kids, would always go for just one more run.

One time I issued a challenge on Duski's behalf. The grandchildren had gotten a couple of new sleds—the latest thing—not just with runners, but also with a comfortable seat, and a steering wheel. A lot fancier and more expensive than the molded plastic sleds and saucers they already had. But were they faster? I didn't think so.

As Emily, Brian, David and Jay got ready for their first run, I said, "I'll bet Duski can beat these sleds to the bottom without half trying."

"Uh-uh," Emily shook her head emphatically, "I bet she can't."

"If she does," I said, making up the rules, "you have to pull Duski back up the hill on the sled."

The children laughed, and Duski's ears perked up as she swung around to look at me excitedly. She was eager to get started. I knew from her expression that those sleds didn't have a chance and Duski was about to get her first ride, ever, up the hill. Age was catching up to the little dog, but not yet enough to overtake her competitive spirit.

She flew down the hill, her tiny black body almost disappearing between her rapid leaps through the deep snow. It was no contest, those sleds were a lot slower than the old ones. When Emily finally reached the bottom, where

Duski waited, panting happily and resting on her haunches, she ceremoniously lifted the little dog into the driver's seat.

Duski looked like a princess, sitting regally upright, as Emily pulled and Brian pushed. Jay and David were lying in the snow, half way down the hill, after running into each other. Those days were long, and physically exhausting for us all, but quite wonderful, as is the memory now.

When the late afternoon sun tinted the snow to colors of gold, the children and dogs piled into our kitchen to warm up. As the children peeled off their ice encrusted snowsuits, and put their mittens on the heater, I fixed hot chocolate for them, and warm milk for Duski and Blaze.

In the summer, at the beach, the children all took turns walking Duski on a leash. Sometimes they'd drag her, when she went too slow, preoccupied with sniffing. Other times, she'd take off following a scent, or chasing a seagull, and pull the unsuspecting grandchild to his or her knees. Duski wasn't too good on a leash. She was more of a "free-spirit."

For Jack's son, Christopher, Duski was more than a playmate. She was—well—she was like an older sibling watching over him from the time he was seven years old.

The years following Jody's suicide, and then after the house fire, were particularly difficult for the boy. Duski's comfort and reassurance were much needed, and always there. Our house, at night, could be a scary place for a child. The old farm house moaned with the night wind—the

Duski's Story

floors and timbers creaked—the hollow walls echoed with scampering mice during the winter's cold. The little boy would call out for the little dog and when she came, and leaped onto his bed and into his arms, his fears were calmed and he'd sleep through the night. Duski seemed to understand, and never left his side. She slept, bound in his arms, the covers over her body and head.

But Duski also needed similar reassurance. Thunderstorms had never frightened her. But after the death of all her puppies, except Blaze, in our house fire that was caused by a lightning strike, thunderstorms terrified her. If a storm swept in during the day, she'd immediately find one of us, and insist upon being held. She'd curl up in my lap, or Jack's, shuddering with fear until the storm passed. Obviously the memories of her tragedy, of death, were as vivid and painful as my own.

If a storm struck at night, Duski would leave her bed on the floor and hop onto our bed. The sudden intrusion always roused us and we'd look to see our little dog sitting on the bed nervously staring from one to the other, silently pleading to be allowed to stay where she knew she wasn't supposed to be. We never refused, but she always waited for permission. "It's okay Duski," we'd say, "come in," as we patted the space between us, where she quickly nestled in, her frightened quivering subsiding, but not leaving until the storm did.

At first, I suppressed the questions Duski's behavior suggested, but eventually I allowed myself to think about how her loss and trauma were so similar to what I experienced because of my loss of Jody.

Those thoughts deepened as Duski became even more attentive during the writing of my first book, *Everything To Live For*, about Jody's suicide, and the lessons I had learned, and the warnings for other parents and teens. That book was written in long-hand—several drafts—endless changes, all with a pen and numerous spiral notebooks. It took me three years of writing, at night, on weekends, vacations and holidays, because I was still working ten to twelve hour days at the TV station. I wrote sitting on my bed at home and on the beach in Ocean City. Duski never left my side during the entire time. Reading passages to her seemed appropriate—for she seemed like my collaborator. I held her close and cried when re-living, as I wrote, the events leading up to Jody's suicide. She seemed to understand and licked away the tears so I could go on.

Duski was helping me say all the things that Jody was unable to talk about when he was going through them, to provide lessons that would help other teens and their parents avoid our pain. I felt that the story had to be written; perhaps it was part of my mission for this lifetime. But was it also Duski's?

CHAPTER ELEVEN
Ocean City, Maryland
1984

Duski and Blaze are trotting along the edge of the ocean. Jack and I follow them. We breathe deeply, drawing in the salt air. It's good to be here, even if we've come to work.

Waiting for me, back in the condo, lying on the kitchen counter, in a big brown envelope with a New York postmark, is the returned manuscript that the editor has gone over and marked up. The publisher who has bought the rights to the book plans to release it in hardback, nine months from now, with a nationwide book tour. I need to have the revisions back in just two months.

At home, when I received it, I scanned it quickly. Seeing the margins crowded with comments and questions, I put it away until I could give it my full attention, here at the beach. Jack, who helped me edit and write the book originally, will help me now go over the changes the editor wants.

Jack stretches, getting ready for his run. "I won't be long," he says, as he and Blaze take off down the beach.

Blaze has become Jack's running partner. Duski, who has trouble staying focused on just running, and tends to stop and sniff, stays with me.

We sit by a dune, I lean back against the snow fence, brushing the sand from Duski's coat and out of her eyes. Her whiskers and eyebrows are now laced with grey. "You're too young for grey hair," I smile. "You should do what I do. No tell-tale grey for me, not if I want to be on television." Her grey fringed eyes look dubious as she licks my hand.

The sun is warm. I'm not ready to work; I just want to be lazy, lie out on the beach and get tanned. I'm tired. "Maybe there isn't so-o-o much work, maybe it just looks like a lot," I say aloud. Duski looks at me intently; sympathetically. "It'll be all right," I reassure, talking as much to myself as the dog. "We'll make it through. We've gotten through much tougher things, haven't we girl?"

Not far from where we sit is the beach house that Jack and I rented the last summer Jody was alive, August 1976. It is a tall, narrow, two story, frame house built on pilings; painted misty green. The owners call it "The Feathered Serpent." It has a prime location, ocean front, and in spite of encroaching development, some sand dunes remain on the right side of its large lot. When we rented it eight years ago, it was entirely surrounded by protective dunes, thick with the tall dune grasses of undeveloped shoreline.

We were all there that summer, even Marjorie's dog Jackson, our last family vacation with Jody.

I look down at Duski, and stroke her head. I turn to gaze out at the ocean and realize that it's not the work I'm dreading. It's that I don't want to go back, yet again. I don't want to reopen that wound one more time. I'm not sure I can. I've got to allow myself to heal. I've got to stop thinking about the pain—what happened and why. I've got to go on. Why did I want to write this book anyway? Why did it seem so important?

Duski climbs onto my lap, looking up at my face. "Well, you're so smart—why?" She licks my chin and makes me smile. "You'd tell me if you could—wouldn't you? You probably know." Her eyes search my face, not as if she's trying to understand what I'm saying, but as if she does. "Remember the first time you saw that beach house?" Her eyes never leave mine. "I sure do."

It had been during Duski's first visit to Ocean City—our first time back after Jody's death—and we were staying at the rented condo. It was the time we came without Duski because pets weren't allowed, but then Jack drove home to get her because I was so unhappy. As soon as Duski arrived, excitedly, we rushed up onto the beach to show it to her for the first time; only to watch as she raced out onto the sand like a gleeful child returning to a familiar vacation spot. And then, spying the beach house, a block away, she raced ahead, bounding up the long stairs to the deck, sniffing and whining at the sliding glass door, scratching at it to get in. No one was staying there then, but even now, she never passes the house without checking to see who's there and if they'll let her in.

"You love that house, don't you?" I say, looking into Duski's eyes, who is now sitting upright in my lap, alert, paying attention to what I'm saying. "I do too. I wish we could afford to buy it. I'd really fix it up for you. But there's no way."

A shadow falls across my face. Duski jumps down off my lap as I look up. "Okay kid, let's go," Jack says. "It's time to get started."

There isn't one page that isn't marked—not one. Almost every margin on every page is crammed with questions and suggestions. "What was his expression? What tone of voice did he use? What time of day was it? What were you thinking when he said this?"

Thumbing through the pages I stop and read one of the editor's questions. "Why do you think your son shouldn't have committed suicide? You were busy with your career—you were involved with Jack—his father was gone—what reasons did he have to want to live?"

The questions seem rude, insensitive. I feel defensive and hurt. I've given this all I have, and now she wants more. I thought she understood.

"I can't do any more," I say with tears, as I hand the page to Jack. "I thought she knew how much I loved Jody—what I've been through—why I'm doing this."

I'm frustrated, hurt and angry, "I won't do any more." I drop the manuscript in the wastebasket and leave the apartment, now rushing blindly to the beach.

Jack follows, walking beside me without saying anything. His presence calms; the anger subsides leaving only the hurt.

Several blocks down the beach he speaks; softly, just above a whisper. "She might understand. She's talked with you in person— she's seen the pain on your face and in your eyes— heard the regrets and remorse in your voice. What she's saying with those questions is that if you don't explain it properly to the readers they won't see and hear what she did. They won't understand, and then they won't care. And if they don't care about you and Jody, the book will be worthless— it won't do what you want it to do."

The truth of his words ease the hurt. He's right— she's right. I must find a way to explain what I think went wrong, so that others might be spared.

We walk, both of us deep in thought, back to the condo. Duski and Blaze greet us. But Duski has pages of the manuscript in her mouth, that she pulled from the trash can. She brings them to me. I look at Jack, "I guess I'm outnumbered."

CHAPTER TWELVE
The Beach
2001 – The Present

For this year's visit to our rented beach house in Delaware, I have set up my writing station angled in the windowed south/east corner of the big front bedroom on the second floor. When I'm not concentrating on the words, displayed on the screen in front of me, I can look out in three different directions. I can watch the sun follow its daily path, sliding up from behind the dark edge of infinity, between ocean and sky, slowly passing overhead until it gradually descends behind this house and disappears into Rehoboth Bay. The setting sun's reflected light colors the waves, and the long empty stretches of glossy wet sand, a luminous pink.

Periodically I gaze down the beach to study a lonely figure walking his dog, or up the beach as a hooded image backpedals against the northeast winds that blow more frequently in the off-season.

Where I write is important to me, because I tend to stare more than create. But when I do write, the words come more easily when my eyes can feast on such scenes by just lifting my head. Here it's the tides, and the wind, moving the beach as well as the ocean. At home, on the farm, it's a landscape of fields and woods and the creatures that pass quietly through without disruption; the birds, a red fox, an occasional deer.

It helped to write *Everything To Live For* at the beach where Jody had spent time, and on our farm, where he lived and died. Somehow, those places allowed me to reconstruct his life; gave me permission to write what was private and often painful.

That book did open our personal lives to the public, and not everyone in the family was pleased about that, including my mother, although, she did tell me that she understood why I wrote it. I hope Jody would have too. Duski certainly seemed to reflect my pleasure that it was widely read and touched many lives. A nationwide book tour took me to fourteen cities in sixteen days, putting our story before thousands of people through newspaper articles, radio shows and national television programs such as "Regis Philbin," "Oprah" and "Good Morning America."

At the end of the interview on "Good Morning America," David Hartman said to me, "Susan, you look as if you want to say something else—we only have 15 seconds left—but what is it."

I quickly said, "If someone is thinking that their life isn't worth living, that nobody cares—I beg them to wait until tomorrow. Things can change, and often do. And tomorrow they may want to live."

The next day I was back in Baltimore, being interviewed on "People Are Talking," a TV talk show that also took phone calls, and was hosted by Richard Sher. It was the show that Oprah had co-hosted with Richard, and which sent her on her way to Chicago and her own show.

About halfway through the program, they took a call from a viewer who said, "I just wanted Susan to know that I was going to kill myself yesterday. I had a bottle of pills in my hand— the TV was on to "Good Morning America" and I heard what she said and I threw the pills in the toilet. I just called to tell her she was right. Today I'm glad I didn't do what I was going to do yesterday. Today I'm glad I'm still alive." In the ensuing years I've received many similar messages; helping others to avoid such pain has helped ease my own. Writing has been the path— the connection— for healing, and I think, especially for me, for understanding.

It's Christmas eve at the beach, and the view outside the windows of my writing station has turned stormy. A twelve-foot pine tree, planted in the sand, decorated with red bows and white lights, is surrounded by the white foam of a churning ocean, which at high tide seems to be chal-

Returning

lenging the decorated tree's right to be there. The electric cord, attached to the string of lights, runs under the sand, through the dunes, to an elegant ocean front beach house. The tree is a gift from the owners of that house to those of us who have chosen the roar of the waves instead of sleigh bells or mall music this year.

Christmases have become quiet occasions for Jack and me; a time to reflect, and enjoy the company of each other. Our grown children who once all lived nearby are now scattered. The grandchildren are practically grown and moving about between colleges and family. With retirement, and the off-season rental of this beach house, we have discovered the peace of solitude, even on holidays.

Family Christmases, when Duski was alive, grew to be momentous times, the memories of which I treasure. As the years passed, and the family expanded, through marriages and grandchildren, the celebrations became grander, so different from the first Christmas after Jody's death, which was tragically bleak.

My sadness, that first Christmas, was expressed by resentment that others didn't seem to grieve as deeply as I. I had tried and failed to make Christmas the same as before. It wasn't; it couldn't be; it never would be. The presents and the tree without joy; the meal without taste. Jack and Christopher had left to visit family—better they go. Marjorie was in California—better she be there. O'Donnell was home, but with a mother so missing the child who had died, that she couldn't enjoy the one who was alive—better she find friends.

    The house, penetrated by the winter's chill, was also empty of human warmth. The floors underfoot were cold as I walked from room to room; the old, un-insulated window panes barely held back the wind. Patiently, the little dog followed as I roamed throughout, then walked with me as I climbed the stairs to the third floor. She watched as I stretched across his bed; leaving me to my pain; waiting for it to ebb. Perhaps, sensing that I needed to face these feelings alone, she curled up on a red and black wool shirt jacket that had fallen to the floor from a chair in the corner of the room, over by the window. Or had she pulled it down to make a bed? Sitting up, abruptly, my eyesight blurred by tears, the bright vision before me was wavering, like the stained glass of a church window illuminated by the sun, only this was more beautiful then any I'd ever seen. The soft afternoon rays filtering in were spotlighting the black dog on the red and black jacket; the red bleeding into the black, and the scene encircled by a halo of gold. Duski had fallen asleep on a Christmas gift I'd given to Jody the year before, his last Christmas on earth with his family. If ever I've felt the hand of God it was then.

    After that first Christmas, the joy of giving returned. When I began to feel cheated that Jody wasn't there to buy for, I'd buy an extra gift, that I might have bought for him,

DUSKI'S STORY

and give it to one of the others, without telling them that it had been intended for Jody. I also bought many gifts for Duski; often things she not only didn't need, but didn't want, such as a little red doggy sweater. When I put the Christmas sweater on her, and took a picture, her expression clearly told me that she was only allowing herself to wear this silly thing to please me. And she reminded me of Jody. He hated clothes that made him stand out, that he thought were too bright, too fussy, or inappropriate. As a small boy, he didn't even like wearing costumes on Halloween. I took the sweater off Duski and quietly promised her that she could use it to play with, chew up or sleep on, but I wouldn't make her wear it, ever again.

Out of the window the tide has subsided and I watch as a man wearing a ret hat, with two black dogs, red ribbons tied around their necks, walk onto the beach. They circle the Christmas tree in the sand; he checks, and finds it secure; lashed tightly to a post. The dogs check the smells, find more than pine, and add to it. It's a Christmas attraction for all who pass by.

I watch the dogs as they play and am reminded, not only of the companionship dogs provide for us, but, of what they can mean to each other.

It was when Marjorie, her first husband and their dog Jackson moved back to the farm, from California, in the early 1980s, that Duski seemed most content with her life, and remained so from then on. The tragic loss caused by the house fire was past. The joy she obtained from the obvious love for and closeness with her daughter, Blaze, and with us her human family was apparent. It would seem that she had the family just the way she wanted it. And it was then that Blaze and Jackson became close, with Duski's parental supervision and consent, of course. Duski never surrendered her role as Blaze's mother or playmate, but she did allow the huge male Doberman to join in their rough-housing, that is unless his size and strength became overpowering. When that happened, Duski would jump at Jackson and bark, the angry tone of which always made him back off and stop. He would even leave the area if Duski persisted, apparently letting him know that she had decided that the play was over for that day. She would then lead Blaze back inside, or off somewhere else on their own. Duski was small, but she was in charge around here.

Eventually, however, with Duski's permission, Jackson and Blaze formed a bond that was never broken until Jackson's death. Since Blaze was spayed, it was a platonic relationship; perhaps all the stronger because it was based solely on mutual respect, companionship, and a common interest.

Every morning Jackson would come to the sliding glass door of our bedroom and scratch on the glass, inviting Blaze to come out and play. Blaze would immediately run to the door, yelping with anticipation, until we opened it. The two dogs would excitedly sniff each other and then nuzzle noses before running off into the woods around the reservoir for the rest of the day. Duski showed no jealousy—perhaps even understanding that it was time for her daughter to have a life apart from her, and knowing that Blaze would be safe with Jackson while she spent the day with me. And in the evening she and her daughter reunited in their ritual of fun and affection.

As I sit in this window and write I can't help but remember that I was writing, working on my third book, when

Duski's Story

Duski's life was beginning to come to an end. Her little body seemed to be wearing out. Her spirit was still strong, her eyes bright and knowing, but a physical weakness was setting in. It was in May of 1990, exactly thirteen years after Jody's suicide that I took her to the vet and was told that her kidneys were failing; that she'd have a little more time, but not much—maybe a couple of months.

I had left television by then and was home almost every day, so we were constantly together. By now Jack and I rarely used the upstairs, except for overnight guests, or grandchildren. But after leaving television I set up an office for myself in one of the upstairs rooms. There is an outside entrance, stairs and door, but the only inside access is a narrow, custom-made, wooden, spiral staircase similar to the metal ones you find backstage in theaters. We had the same kind of staircase at the television station, going from the studio floor to the director's booth.

Duski and Blaze could easily get up the outside stairs, but neither one of them ever attempted to climb the narrow, slippery, winding one on the inside. Sometimes I'd escort them both up from the outside, and often I'd carry Duski up from the inside. But as Duski's illness progressed she only seemed comfortable in her doggy bed in our bedroom, and I'd just leave her there. Blaze had a bed there as well and I figured they were company for each other, and better off there for the few hours I was upstairs.

One day, as I wrote intently on the word processor, I heard a sound, as I turned to see what it was—I was stunned. Duski! Her pace was painfully slow, almost dragging herself across the room, then crawling under the table, where I was working, and curling up at my feet. She had somehow managed to pull herself up the spiral staircase to be with me. I never left her alone again.

In early summer I took her to the vet once more to see if there was anything else I could do, or should do, to prolong her life, or ease her pain.

"Try to keep water in her," the vet said, "and try to get her to eat at least a little something each day."

Duski was getting very thin.

"Kidney failure," he went on, is not a quick or easy death. You might want to think about putting her to sleep. She's not going to get better."

Tears filled my eyes. I shook my head because I could not speak. I picked up my little dog and held her close. Walking to the car I whispered to her. "Not this time Duski. I'll stay with you—it'll be all right. We'll face your death together—the natural way."

CHAPTER THIRTEEN
The Farm
Summer 1990

I put my finger in the bowl of water and moisten her mouth with it. She licks it from her lips without lifting her head. Any movement is difficult. She doesn't want to eat, and it's hard now to make her drink. I've tried using an eyedropper, but even that much water makes her choke. She doesn't seem to be in pain, she's just weak. I know her life is slipping away.

"It's okay Duski—for you to go—it's okay." I speak as softly and as reassuringly as I can. "You'll be okay," Her eyebrows twitch as she looks up at me. She looks as concerned for me as I am for her. "I'll be okay too—don't worry about me."

I pick her up in my arms and carry her out by the pool. Blaze follows and settles nearby. I sit in a lounge chair in the shade, holding Duski on my lap. I can feel her heart. It's weak, and erratic. Her legs jerk. "It's okay—I love you." I smooth the wiry hair back over her emaciated body. It's like stroking a skeleton covered with fur.

"You've had a good life and you've lived it well." I go on petting as I talk. "You've been a good mother." I reach over to pet Blaze, who looks worried and sad. I return my attention to Duski, "You helped get Jack and me together—you pulled us all together—the whole family. You helped Christopher grow up—you know that, don't you?" She licks my hand. "You were there for Marjorie and O'Donnell. You certainly helped raise the grandchildren. And we had fun, too, didn't we girl? Fun here on the farm—fun at the beach—fun when we traveled; California—our second trip there, that was the best, remember when we all went on to Hawaii after O'Donnell's graduation from college?"

I smile, thinking of how we smuggled Duski into restaurants and hotels where dogs weren't allowed, and on the cable cars in San Francisco. I'd put her in a big beach bag, or inside my coat. No one, but us, knew she was there, except when she stuck her head out to catch the breeze as the trolley sped down the hills of San Francisco.

I kiss the top of her head and continue to talk, thinking she can understand me, certain she finds the sound of my voice comforting.

"But you didn't like those Hammerhead sharks on the beach in Maui, did you? None of us did. I'll never forget that old toothless fisherman pulling in those nets filled with those sharks. I was yelling that he shouldn't throw them back in the ocean—you were barking because I was yelling—and he was laughing at us both, saying 'They're just babies—they won't hurt you—there're plenty others out there.' And then we saw their huge mother leap out of the water just off shore. That did it for us—didn't it? After that, we all just stayed by the pool."

I fall silent with my thoughts, as I go on stroking my little companion. Speaking again my voice is now just above a whisper. "I loved it when you could travel with us. Everything was more fun with you—my life more complete. You know that, don't you girl?"

Duski's tail wags ever so slightly. "You do know what I'm saying don't you—every word. You must also know what you've accomplished in this lifetime—in these thirteen years.

For one, you stayed with me and made sure I wrote that book. Didn't give me a minute's rest, for three years, until it was done. And you were right. You know that don't you?"

Duski's head remains still, but her eyes move to connect with mine. Then they move away staring at something in the distance, or perhaps focusing on something she sees with her mind's eye.

My words are now choked with emotion. "I forgive you—you know—that pain." Her eyes dart back and lock on mine. "I do—I love you so much—I always did." Her eyes move slowly away. I pause, hesitant—"Do you forgive me?" With what little strength remains she lifts her head slightly off my lap. Her soulful eyes penetrate my heart. I want to erase the words. "I know you do—you wouldn't have returned if you didn't." Her head drops, her body lays limp. "It's all right," I repeat again. "And I'll be all right—I know your work is done—I'll miss you—but I'll be all right—this time."

I touch my hand to Duski's nose, it's dry. Her body seems cool. There's now a faraway look in her eyes.

"It's okay Duski—don't worry about leaving me," I repeat. "I'll be okay." With her head averted I hope she can no longer see the tears spilling down my cheeks, tears that betray my words.

I pick her up and carry her carefully back inside. Blaze follows. Standing over Duski's bed I kiss her on the back of the neck as I kneel to put her down. I turn and walk to the sliding glass door, staring out—trying to hide my emotion from Duski. The hurt I feel is more than I have felt since... Feeling her brush against my leg I look down.

Somehow she's found the strength to lift herself off the bed and come back to me. My vision of her is blurred by more tears as I bend to stroke her.

Duski looks up at me for a long moment and then turns and walks back to her bed. I follow and speaking softly of my love I feel her last breath. She is gone. It's over.

CHAPTER FOURTEEN
The Farm
2001

I sprinkle some fish food on the little pond we created on the south side of the farm house next to the screened-in porch, and watch the bright orange goldfish surface with their mouths open in motion to feed. I glance over to the nearby bank where Duski is buried under the Japanese black pine. In the years since, I've planted lilies, mint, wild strawberries, and forget-me-nots that now cascade to the water's edge.

The grandchildren, each in their own thoughtful way came to say goodbye to Duski when she died. They were so young then; all under 10 years of age. Emily, the oldest, is now in college. Before the burial they came with flowers, and one brought a dog biscuit (in case Duski got hungry on her way to heaven). She was buried with one of their toys and her old red Christmas sweater, that I tucked under her head as a pillow. I didn't think she'd mind it that way.

Without telling anyone what it was, I wrapped her body in an old flannel blanket that I had torn in half. I still have the other half. It was Jody's security blanket when he was a baby.

I kept it folded in the bottom of a drawer with some other items that were special to him, and are now treasures to me. One is the bright yellow shirt with his name on the back that he wore to race moto-cross.

Jack and the children said their goodbyes. We all grieved and didn't even try to hold back the tears, but none of us grieved more than Duski's daughter, Blaze, re-enforcing my belief that a dog's emotions can run as deeply as ours.

We buried Duski on her doggy bed that had been in our bedroom. Blaze wasn't aware that it had been removed, because she refused to come into the room. She had seen Duski die there. When Jack finally coaxed Blaze into the room to go to her bed she saw that Duski's bed was gone, and she stopped—frozen—just staring at that spot. Then she turned, abruptly, and did something she had never done before—she went into Jack's closet, sat and just stared at the wall. We tried to coax her out, but she refused and spent the night in that closet. The next night we got her to use her doggy bed, but she wouldn't face where Duski had been, as she always had before. Instead, she slept with her back to that spot—for the rest of her life.

Blaze lived only two years longer and I don't think her zest for life was ever quite the same, she too is buried by the fish pond, next to her mother.

This spring, May of 2002, will be the twenty-fifth anniversary of my son Jody's death and this coming summer will be the same anniversary of Duski's appearance. I've gone on with my life, but Jody is in my thoughts every day and I think of Duski almost as often—because they seem so connected.

I've spent hours reflecting on Duski's life as it related to Jody's. It all made sense to me; the spiritual return of my son in the form of the little dog. The relationship I had with Jody, and then with Duski. I've thought about the karma and the lessons he would have learned.

Coming back as a female, Jody experienced the joys of motherhood. But with the house fire he experienced what it is like to have an offspring die; of having a life you gave birth to, nurtured and loved, suddenly taken from you. Having experienced that kind of pain yourself you would never want to impose such pain willingly on a parent. In any other future life suicide would never be an option again.

Those people, who believe, say that karma is always fair; that what you impose on people in one lifetime you must experience in another.

As a shy teenager Jody could not speak of his feelings—of a broken home, the death of his father, seeing his mother falling deeply in love with someone else—wanting to be part of that relationship, of having a real family, but not being able to show it or speak of it.

I believe Duski learned the value of communicating, by staying by my side for the three years I analyzed, and wrote, and talked to her about Jody's life and suicide; sorting out what went wrong and why. Duski gave her support, helped me through it and she could see how it helped me, and the reactions of others it helped.

Jody's love for me, and for all of his family, was unconditional, even though that love was not rewarded with the security of a solid family, that was always there for him. Jody hated to be left alone—Duski almost never was. Certainly Duski helped bring us all together to become the close family Jody always wanted.

As I now think about the two lives, I recall my visit in 1994 to karmic astrologer Linda Brady. Her voice clear, her words then seem to verify my thoughts now about Duski's life coming from Jody's spirit, and the karma it carried.

Reading from his chart she said, "Jody was your soul mate. You had known each other in many lifetimes. Jody had two soul missions for his short life. He needed to understand mother, and that kind of love, and he needed to awaken you to the powerful emotions of your soul mission, revealed in your north node of Scorpio—investigating the depth of your emotions and how to use them for self-healing, and for helping others—transforming darkness into light."

Did Duski continue Jody's mission as my soul mate: to understand mother and that kind of love; being with me constantly for such and important period of my life. And from her own perspective; giving birth to the puppies, losing all but one in the house fire, then going on, after tragedy, with her daughter Blaze. Duski's example of being a good mother, under similar circumstances, was one to follow; experiencing the devastation of losing offspring, but spending the rest of her life being devoted to the one she had left. Linda's voice comes back, and seems haunting. "You gave Jody a good idea of what love is—in his next life he'll remember that."

And if Jody had a mission to awaken me I would say that Duski continued it.

Linda's voice returns, "If Jody comes back he'll come back for you, Mom."

And yet something was still gnawing at me, something not quite right—not something Linda said, but something she didn't say.

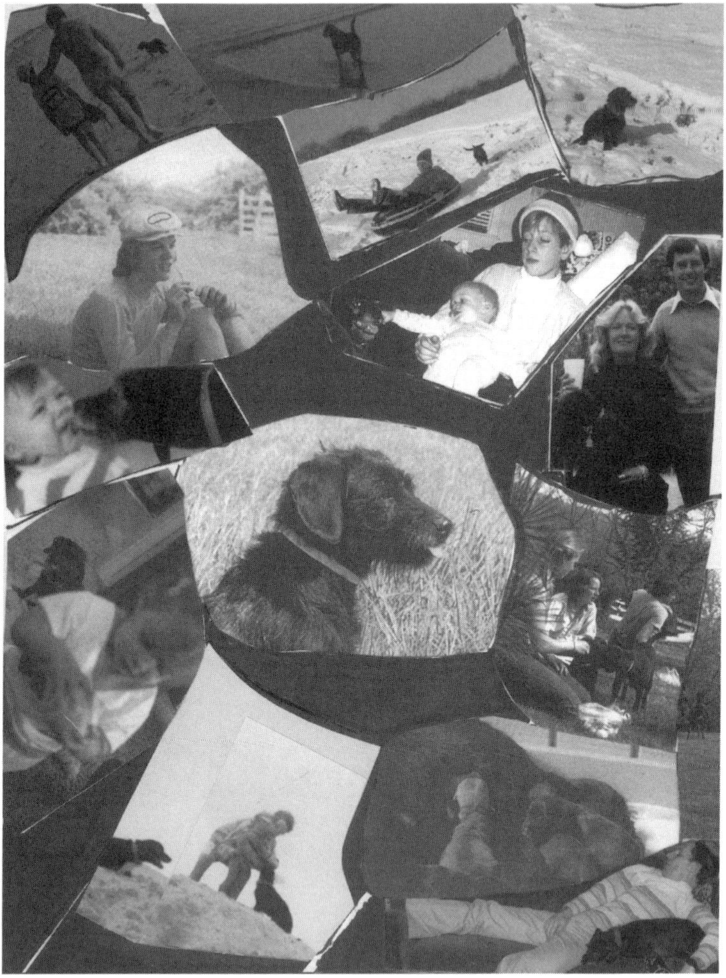

CHAPTER FIFTEEN
September 2002

It took me almost a year to call for my second appointment with Linda Brady. Almost a year of thinking about my question; pretty sure what her answer would be—that she would cast doubt on my suspicions about Duski. I liked my theory and found comfort in thinking that Duski had carried on with Jody's life and his soul mission, completing what Jody had started with me, and even fulfilling the karmic debt he had incurred.

But I knew that very few people in this country, outside of Hollywood, believe in transmigration. Even those who believe very strongly in reincarnation do not believe in spiritual cross-over—that a human spirit, or soul, could return in animal form, or the other way around. However, millions of Buddhist and Hindus do, thus their belief in such beings as "the sacred cow."

Intellectually, I find the whole concept of reincarnation to be implausible, but if a soul does continue from one lifetime into another it seems to me it could just as easily come back in animal form as human.

I could have gone on, accepting my premise, taking comfort in the belief I'd held for twenty-five years, and not gone back to see what Linda thought. I didn't really need someone, anyone, to confirm or dispel my beliefs. However, when I started writing Duski's story it seemed important to see what this highly respected karmic astrologer, who knew Jody's story, would have to say; to get another point of view, not that anyone could know for sure. Aside from that, my spiritual curiosity was peaked, as well as my desire, as a writer, to get that other perspective. And I needed to confront what I hadn't before.

Not much has changed in eight years; not the area in Baltimore where Linda lives, not her house, or her. We both carry a few more pounds, but age usually brings weight, as well as wisdom, and women who are secure about themselves are usually comfortable with all three, so I find that change reassuring.

We hug warmly, exchanging compliments, genuinely glad to see each other. She shows me into the same counseling room as before, saying that she'll be right with me. Things seem the same here as well, although a new dog greets me. A little, high energy Shih-Tzu jumps up on the couch and licks my face. I pet the dog with affection glad to make a new friend.

With the pleasantries out of the way we get to the purpose of my visit. I begin without any urging. "When I was here before, you asked me if I thought I would see Jody again? If I thought he would incarnate during my lifetime? I said I thought he already had, and I went on to say that I thought that the little dog that came to our house after Jody's death was my son reincarnated. You skirted that comment by saying, 'No—I mean in human form.' At the time, I thought about each of my grandchildren, but told you I didn't think he had incarnated as any of them. You said I'd know if Jody returned; that there wouldn't be any doubt in my mind. And there hasn't been. The truth is, I didn't even seriously consider any of the grandchildren, because I was so certain that Jody returned as my little dog, and the dog was alive when all of the grandchildren were born. That's how sure I was that Jody's spirit had come back to me."

Linda looks as though she knows where I'm going, but I go there anyway. "I could tell, by your reaction, that you probably didn't think that could happen; a silly thought not worth talking about, so I let it drop. I wasn't secure enough then to pursue it. I am now. Why didn't you encourage me to talk about the dog and my suspicions that it carried Jody's spirit?"

"Ahhh," Linda sighs displaying empathy, as well as understanding about the reason for my return visit.

"The reason I skirted it is because, in my personal view, I don't believe people return as animals. I think animal spirits are animal spirits and people spirits are people spirits."

"I thought that might be the reason," I say without surprise or disappointment.

"I'm not sure about that," Linda continues, "that's just my personal belief, and I don't like to impose my personal beliefs on anyone."

I'm surprised by this comment, because it seems to me that most of what she teaches about reincarnation, soul contracts and soul connections is based on personal beliefs. None of it can be proven.

I challenge her reasoning, and she elaborates, admitting that there is no proof either way, for any of it. "I just believe that animal spirits are sacred. There's a judgement that animal spirits need to become human spirits for them to be better—for them to be more evolved, or more illuminated, and I just can't buy that. I think animal spirits are very illuminated. To be truthful, sometimes I don't see human spirits quite as illuminating. It's probably very biased, based on my intense love of animals. I just honor them as exactly who and what they are without a need to switch over and become human. Animals often take on the personalities of their owners—that's how they serve us. They show us pieces of ourselves.

"So in that regard people could claim that they're acting like human beings. And they are. Animals have emotions; they have sensibilities; they have intuition; they have all these things, so in that regard they are like us. *But they don't have to be us*, to achieve a better or higher form of life."

Linda pauses before going on. "However, I do think that there are ways that their spirits connect with us."

"Then you do believe that dogs can have a spirit or soul?"

"Of course, but I believe that they have their own place on the other side; that they have their own consciousness. I believe they have *soul contracts* with us, and *know* what they are. I think God has given us dogs, and cats and other animals, that live for a shorter period of time than we do, in order for us to understand that reincarnation exists."

Linda goes on to explain the soul contract she believes she has had with three of her dogs—the same soul in all three dogs. "My first soul dog was Pom. He died May 11, 1977." I feel a physical reaction to this; an internal quiver, because Jody died the same week—May 9, 1977, but I say nothing, letting Linda go on. She points to the little dog now curled up on the floor near my feet, and says to me, "When you were here before that was Ti I, this is Ti II."

I think about the greeting the dog gave me. It was as if he'd seen me before.

"But," I interject, unconvinced by her arguments and hoping she'll be persuaded by the details of Duski's life, "let me tell you about this little dog and the remarkable things she did—the actions and reactions that could have only been motivated by Jody."

Linda listens with animated interest. I tell her about the hat and the motorcycle trail; the puppies and house fire, and the support and patience the dog gave me as I wrote my book about Jody.

Linda eagerly responds, seemingly without pausing for reflection. "You know what this is? This is your son sending you a gift. This is your son saying, 'Okay Mom, I'm fine, I'm cool— here's this gift to you that will be your connection to me— here's this little puppy that's telling you I'm alive, I'm well, I'm fine and through this dog you will heal.' That's what it was, I think. It was his specter on the other side orchestrating this connection." Linda stops, and shivers, "It gives me chills."

Now, Linda does pause to reflect before proceeding. When she finally speaks her words come at a slower, more pronounced pace.

"You see, Susan, it doesn't necessarily have to be Jody's spirit within the dog, but instead, Jody's spirit that created the dog. Do you see the difference?"

I nod, I do see the difference, but I'm not convinced. That concept seems more complicated, more convoluted, in a spiritual sense, than Jody's soul simply returning as Duski.

Linda goes on, with new energy, caught up in the idea of Jody sending this little dog that he had informed about his life and mine. "I think Jody saw your pain. He knew what you were going through and he wanted to find a physical manifestation of love for you—a way—something to help—something that he couldn't do himself. But he could do it through this animal spirit. Jody sent the dog. The dog shows its connection with Jody, through the hat and the motorcycle trail and all the other things, saying, in effect relaying Jody's message: 'Get it, Mom, I'm okay, so you be okay'."

I don't know. The closeness I felt with Duski, the companionship, the dog's attitude, mannerisms, actions and reactions, the experiences with me and Jack and the rest of the family seemed much more like Jody than a messenger sent by him. Besides, I believe that Jody had already sent me that message. I've always believed, and wrote in my book *From A Healing Heart*, that I felt that the single flower, a Black-Eyed-Susan, that grew from the bare dirt on Jody's grave, shortly after his death, *was a* sign from him saying, "I love you Mom, and I'm okay, so you be okay." Jody picked Black-Eyed-Susans for me throughout his life, so I believe that the one on the fresh dirt of his grave had to be from him. But Duski, a sign, a gift from him? I don't know, I still think perhaps she was much more.

I leave Linda's house without resolution.

CHAPTER SIXTEEN
The Beach
October 2002

It's the first week in October and it is as warm as summer. Jack and I have been so lucky with these off-season stays at the beach. I fling a tennis ball out into the ocean, over the first line of breakers, for Angel to retrieve. I'm enjoying using the new contraption called "Chuckit" that my friend Kathy gave me. She read in our book, *Off Season*, that Jack and I co-wrote, that I was using a tennis racquet to hit balls for our dog, thus sparing my throwing arm the strain of trying to throw a distance. She saw the "Chuckit" advertised and thought it would make our beach play even easier and it does. In fact I can now throw even farther than Angel's interest takes her.

Angel trots into the ocean up to her belly and patiently waits for the waves to roll the ball to her. She's gotten very smart about the ways of the ocean during the four years we've been coming here, plus at seven years of age she's also starting to slow down. The truth is, she never has been hyper, even as a young dog. She's always seemed more mature, wiser for her age, perhaps like an only child who's grown up mostly with adults. Here at the beach she fit in right away; comfortable in the beach house and with the rules. She's not allowed on furniture, and we don't let her go upstairs. She tested us a couple of times the first year but never since. Each time, when we arrive, and carry clothes and the baggage upstairs, Angel stays on the first floor, sitting at the bottom of the stairs, waiting for us to come back down. If we take longer than she thinks we should she whines a little, but she never comes up looking for us. She has her bed in the laundry room, and at night a baby gate blocking the doorway ensures she stays put. She seems very content and may not even need the gate.

I go back to the beach chair next to Jack. He's reading so I don't interrupt with conversation. Besides, my thoughts keep returning to my visit with Linda. I'm having trouble thinking about, or concentrating on, anything else. Even when I'm not listening to the tape recording of the session, the conversation keeps replaying in my head. Jack hasn't heard the tape yet, and I haven't told him much of what she said. I will. He'll be patient, but he'll think it's ridiculous, and probably laugh.

Jack puts down his paper and rises from the chair, "I'm going to take Angel for a walk up the beach." Angel looks up at Jack and immediately jumps up, alert and anxious. She knows that word "walk."

"Good," I say, aware that Angel wasn't getting as much exercise as she needed by halfheartedly retrieving balls from the ocean. I'm also glad for the time to think alone.

Angel bounces at Jack's side as they start out. It makes me smile. She does get excited about going for walks. She loves meeting the other dogs on the beach and, just like Duski, she loves sniffing out the identities of those that have been there before her. She drifts toward the snow fencing, nose to the sand, like a bloodhound on the trail, and she periodically leaves her mark, making sure all that follow know she's been there too.

I watch as they move out of sight, past the sparse groupings of October beach sitters on chairs or blankets; some with umbrellas for protection from the unseasonably strong sun. A few have just gratefully plopped onto the sand to soak up that sunshine.

My thoughts return to Angel. We have another wonderful dog that has become an intricate part of our life, our new life in retirement. If the beach house owners hadn't agreed to let us bring a dog with us we wouldn't have had this experience, because we wouldn't have done it without her.

After Blaze died in 1992 neither Jack nor I were very anxious to get another dog, to take on the responsibility of another pet. I enjoyed having them around; in fact I gave the two youngest grandsons, in each family, a dog for their birthdays. Alex got a mixed breed that I found at the Humane Society. He's a mid-sized black dog that looks like a combination of Chesapeake Bay and Labrador Retriever. Alex named him Arrow, because his family already had a dog named Beaux. Then they had Beaux and Arrow.

Tommy got a purebred black lab that he and his family named Memphis Belle. My daughter Marjorie, Tommy's mother, decided it would be fun to have puppies and she bred his dog Memphis to another black lab owned by the man who is the Godfather of Tommy's older brother, Jay.

On March 1, 1995, Memphis gave birth, at home on the farm, and Angel was the first born; a yellow lab of two black lab parents. When I saw the shiny white-gold of this new born pup I said, "Look at that little Angel." There seemed to be a connection right away, and we had a new dog. Jack loves the dog but hates the name I gave her. "Dogs are great protection," he says, "but, 'sick 'em Angel' doesn't sound very threatening."

I do agree with Linda about the importance of dogs in our lives. I pick up the tape recorder by my chair and push the play button, turning down the volume even though no one is close enough to hear. I get lost in her words once more.

"The greatest gifts our pets give us—after love—is an understanding that souls exist—theirs and ours—and that we all return. What better gift is there? None! They are gifts from God; a reflection of God. And people who understand that don't have a lot of fear, or a lot of regrets. They can say good-bye to the people who pass, knowing that they're going to be *re-connected* in a very different way, a better way."

I stop the tape and fast forward to where I was telling Linda about writing Duski's story, and that I still wasn't sure if I wanted it to be published.

She encourages me. "People need to know what animals are to us—how sacred they are and how much they help us to do so many things. Especially this kind of situation—the connection that Jody had with this animal spirit, and the soul contract between you and the dog and your son all coming together to create this healing for you."

I push stop. "I don't know," I think. "Duski, a *gift* from Jody, but not Jody. It's a nice thought, perhaps easier for most people to believe. But not for me. It just isn't strong enough— it doesn't explain everything to my satisfaction."

Linda had argued that animal spirits have a purity of form; possessing the highest manifestation of unconditional love. She contended that to throw them into the human mix would denigrate what they are. And the idea of a human spirit being relegated to animal form as way of punishment, to atone, is abhorrent to her, because she thinks so highly of animals.

But I think about the reverse. I think about a boy, who has displayed unconditional love his entire life; a purity of soul. A shy teenager finding his life so hard to live, so difficult to endure, that he can't. Would it not be a gift, a reward, not punishment, to be given a lifetime without human stress and heartache; to live in a family where he would, without question, *receive* unconditional love from every member of that family; a lifetime void of societal judgement, and one with no concerns about fitting in. And, at the same time, learning some painful karmic lessons, but within a secure, supportive, and loving environment.

Angel, out in front of Jack, leading herself, comes back into view. It's their routine. Jack never uses the leash walking up the beach, letting Angel roam, but staying within sight. When he's ready to start back down the beach he calls her to him and attaches the leash to her collar. Angel gathers the dangling strap off the sand, positions it in her mouth so it doesn't drag, and she won't step on it, then she walks purposefully toward her goal—home. The sight of her walking herself on a leash never fails to get chuckles and comments from the people she passes along the way. Occasionally, seeming to enjoy the attention and praise, she'll stop and let them pet her, as if taking a bow.

When she catches sight of me, Angel begins running and she reaches me at least 100 feet in front of Jack. She stops at my chair, staring intently at my face, waiting for the praise she knows will come. "Good girl, good Angel." I unhook the leash, rub her head with affection, and watch as she walks into the ocean to cool off, ducking her head into the waves, obviously refreshed by the cold salt water washing over her face.

Jack pulls the empty chair into the shade of the umbrella and sits down. He looks happy and relaxed as well. He glances at the tape recorder sitting on the notebook in my lap, the pen in my hand. "How's it going?"

"I don't know, Linda's theory is different from mine." I begin to explain, emphasizing her beliefs that animal spirits are animal spirits and human spirits remain human; that there's no crossover. Jack listens with interest, without showing judgement, and surprisingly without comment. But I shake my head and shrug with the frustration of not being able to feel certain.

Angel walks out of the ocean, back to where I'm sitting. I put my hand out to pet her, gently wiping the water out of her eyes. She sticks her cold wet nose into my face and gives me a big lick right on the mouth. I laugh and turn to Jack, "Using Linda's theory maybe Angel is Duski reincarnated."

"I've always thought that," he says matter-of-factly.

I stare at Jack in astonishment. He smiles, "Well, I don't really believe that—but . . .," and he shrugs. My mind flashes back to the 1994 conversation with Linda. "If Jody had stayed around longer he could have turned Jack around, spiritually."

Angel—Duski—Jody, all connected? Could it be? Can we ever know for sure? Were we meant to know, or simply to guess, and savor the possibilities?

"There are some simple truths...
and dogs know what they are."

Joseph Duemer
Author/Teacher
(b. 1951)

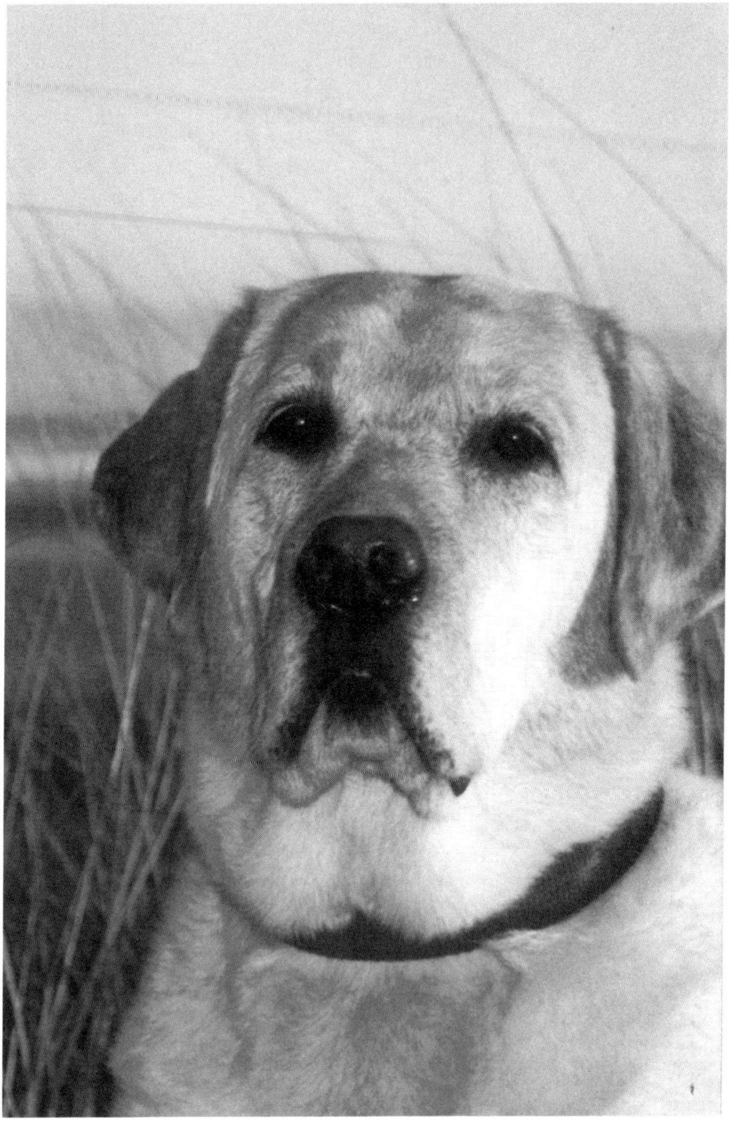

AFTERWORD
About Beliefs:

The simple fact is that there are things about life and death that cannot be explained—some things just need to be accepted as gifts, for what they bring to enrich, enlighten, or empower our existence.

Every major religion, every strong charismatic teacher, throughout the centuries, has felt that their beliefs revealed the meaning and purpose of life; even eternal life. We follow these teachings because they provide what most of us want. Organized religion is a great comfort and guide; a solace for many. Faith is an extraordinarily powerful thing. As a believer in God, a supreme being, I live in awe of the creations that surround us here on earth. I don't understand how anyone can look around at the beauty, the complexity of nature, the power and endurance of the human spirit and not believe in something more powerful than they are.

But even as a believer I also understand that we cannot know for certain. No one can prove heaven or hell, or angels, or reincarnation. No one can guarantee what's on the other side, or if there is another side. But with each spiritual experience, with each relationship that awakens us to understanding or emotion there is reinforcement for our hope that our lives do matter and that the love, the lessons, the compassion will be carried on, perhaps creating more-aware generations to come.

For me, it was the little dog, Duski, that showed me that my son's life was not wasted. Duski taught me that a life, in any form, doesn't have to be long-lasting to have a profound effect. Jody had an important influence on my life and on what I've done with that life. And I know, without question, that his influence and guidance continue with each additional day that I live, and, perhaps will continue beyond. For myself, I hope my soul will provide the same kind of awakening for someone else.

Linda Brady calls herself an Aquarian, a karmic astrologer who believes in God and the teachings of Christ. She says, "I'm a Christian who doesn't follow any dogma."

She believes that Jesus was the son of God, but she also believes that we are all sons and daughters of God. "Jesus said, 'We are all sons of God'," Linda points out.

"I spent most of my young life studying many religions," she says, "Buddhism, Christianity, Judaism, Islam. What I did was look at the similarities of all of the great religions and what I now believe is an amalgamized version of them all.

"It all comes down to love, personal responsibility and divinity. God gave us a soul and in that giving he gave us part of himself. Yes, we are all sons and daughters of God and I believe that we too rise from the dead."

Linda says that astrology is what pulled her beliefs into focus. It's what gave her the meaning she had been looking for. She says that the discovery of that meaning literally saved her life.

"There was a year of my life that I was actively suicidal—and I think I was being quite rational I might add. I was not emotional about it—it was simply a decision that this life wasn't working for me. I didn't like it here and I wanted to go somewhere else. Of course at that point I didn't know where somewhere else was. I just knew I didn't want to be here. So, in essence, coming into astrology really did save my life. Because not only did I find meaning, I found my purpose. And if I hadn't found my purpose, life would have been pretty lackluster for me."

When Linda was 31 years old a series of tragedies led to a dramatic change in her life and put her in position to discover astrology. During a three month period of time she was badly injured in an automobile accident, her surrogate father died, and her marriage ended. Broken on many levels, she suffered a severe depression. She says she wouldn't have wished those three months on her worst enemy, if she had one, and yet that period was the turning point of her life.

Instead of going back to school to earn her doctorate in psychology, which is what she had been planning before the accident, when she recovered she returned to a job at an institution for the mentally handicapped, eventually becoming vice principal of the school there. It was also there that she met her husband, Michael, a man she now calls her soul mate. And she learned astrology. The life she had been ready to discard now had real meaning and purpose.

She has also learned that seeking perfection in life, in this world, is a waste of time. "We need to strive," she says, "not for perfection, but to do the best we can do." She says this is not a perfect plane and never will be.

"There's still a part of me that doesn't like it here," Linda explains, citing how people can abuse each other, animals and the environment. But she accepts the limitations of this life. "I realize that God created this plane to be as it is and this is not the easiest plane to live on—it's actually the most difficult one. So there will be war and there will be hatred and cruelty. It's our reaction to all those things that matters. So finding astrology, and now karmic astrology, saved my life physically and emotionally and certainly spiritually.

"I've had problems with relationships and then finally figuring out what the contracts were—it made so much sense. You see I'm a Sagittarian and before I can teach anything I have to have a personal experience.

"My religious beliefs, like any other, cannot be proven. The only way we can even begin to prove the validity of astrology is through an inductive method—of creating a sample of people and tracking the process of each. But, even then, the nay-sayers are going to have all kinds of reasons why it's not possible.

"It works for me—my personal quest to find meaning was accomplished. And I have seen it work for many, many other people. They bring me thousands of situations, looking for help to find meaning, a reason why these things happen. And that's what I do."

FINAL WORD
The Farm
Winter 2004

As I make the last changes in this book, editing, making corrections, before sending the manuscript back to the publisher, we are back on the farm for the winter after another glorious fall season at the beach. While there, gazing out over the ocean, into the colors of some beautiful sunrises and sunsets, and after considerable reflection, I decided that I would allow this book to be published—allow this story to be told. And now I work to finish it.

It has been a cold and snowy January/February in this year of 2004, and so I don't regret spending some time indoors at this task. My office is now on the first floor, in what was originally built as the den, when my first husband and I added the wing onto the farmhouse right before Jody was born. It's located off of the new open kitchen and dining room area that Jack and I had done in 2001. It's a very convenient place to work and, with the stone fireplace, very cozy this time of year, with this kind of weather.

RETURNING

Curled up on the floor by my desk is "Angel." She's been staying very close as I work. Of course, it could be because it is so comfortable in here, or just perhaps she wants to see me through the process of telling this story, as Duski seemed to do with my first book. Certainly, I cannot know, but for whatever reason I'm encouraged by her closeness. I just thought you'd like to know.

Author Recommended Books

DISCOVERING YOUR SOUL MISSION (How To Use Karmic Astrology To Create The Life You Want) by Linda Brady & Evan St. Lifer.

NO MORE GOODBYES, a True Story, by Linda Brady, Jane Landis and Marty Humphreys.

AN OPEN HEART (Practicing Compassion in Everyday Life) by The Dali Lama published in 2001.

GOOD LIFE, GOOD DEATH (Tibetan Wisdom of Reincarnation) by Rimpoche Nawang Gehlek.

AWAKENING THE BUDDHIST HEART (Integrating Love, Meaning, and Connection into every part of your life) by Lama Surya Das.

LIVING BUDDA/LIVING CHRIST by Thich Nhat Nanh, which is not specifically about reincarnation, but the similarity of the two men and the religious teachings they are given credit for. He says, "When you are a truly happy Christian, you are also a Buddhist. And vice versa." But he also writes about some early Christian beliefs of reincarnation.

OLD SOULS: The Scientific Evidence for Past Lives by Washington Post Journalist and Editor Tom Shroder, which is about the research of Dr. Ian Stevenson of the University of Virginia.

The American Indians were the first in our Western culture to believe in the spirit world and reincarnation. As those beliefs and the beliefs of Eastern cultures, such as Buddhist, have become of popular interest among many people in today's American society the Spiritual sections of book stores and libraries have become filled with books pertaining to the subject. A very simple explanation of the history and beliefs about reincarnation was done by Gary Blackwood in a Benchmark Book titled Long Ago Lives.

I also read *Reincarnation/ A Critical Examination* by Paul Edwards. This is a thoroughly researched, completely scientific, often humorous, and totally sanctimonious book that seems to disprove any possibility of reincarnation, as well as all other spiritual beliefs of any religion that can't be proven through a show and tell methodology. So passionate is his disbelief that I find it sad, because I fear his life must be completely void of the awe and wonder that the rest of us call "the mysteries of life."

Picture Information
& Identification

Page iii	The Beach
Page 4	Duski on the farm 1981
Page 12	Angel at the beach 2001
Page 14	Duski on the beach 1981
Page 38	Puppies 1979
Page 50	Duski and Blaze - pastel drawings by Judy Gibson
Page 66 & Back Cover	Dewey Beach at sunset 2001
Page 70	Top Left: Duski, daughter Marjorie, grandson Jay Easter late 1980s
	Top Right: Daughter O'Donnell, Duski, stepson Christopher Christmas 1980
	Bottom: Duski, Jay, David, Brian, Emily Before Sled Race
Page 73	Jack & Christopher with Duski 1978
Page 80	Beach House – Ocean City, Md. 1976
Page 86	Christmas Tree on Dewey Beach
Page 89	Duski's Christmas Sweater 1980 Blaze & Jackson in background
Page 92	Jackson 1980

Page 104 Pieces of the Puzzle:
JODY 1960-1977 DUSKI 1977-1990
Six Puppies 1 month 1979
Surviving Puppy BLAZE 1979-1992
Clockwise: Family & Companionship:
Walking the beach 1983 – Snow fun 1984 – Christopher in Santa hat, grandson Brian petting Duski 1985 – Loving Parents: Susan & Jack with Duski in Hawaii 1980 – Blaze and Duski with family and friends on Easter 1981 – Jack and Duski on New Year's Eve 1984 – Siblings: Grandchildren: Family Support: Motherhood: Generations: Duski, Blaze, Christopher & Emily at the beach 1984 – Duski in back of granddaughter Emily 1984 and licking grandson Jay 1986.

Page 122 Angel 2002
Page 130 Angel at Peace 2004